THELMA'S TREASURES

The Secret Recipes of
"The Best Cook in Harrodsburg"

by Susanna Thomas

LITTLE BARTER PRESS

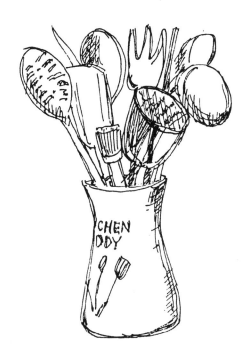

Thelma's Treasures, The Secrets of "The Best Cook in Harrodsburg,"
Requests for permission should be addressed to Little Barter Press, 465 Balden Lane, Harrodsburg, KY 40330.

Fifth printing

Printed in the United States of America
by Little Barter Press
ISBN 0-9638478-8-0

Designed by Virginia Evans
Illustrations by Larrie Curry

Acknowledgments

In writing this cookbook over the last three years, my knowledge (and my husband's waistline) have expanded. I can now make a melt-in-your-mouth turkey and an irresistible whipped cream pound cake. I have learned that dough must only be rolled from the center out, and that simmering green beans should not be stirred. I now know that White Russets are the preferable potato for salad, and that men don't like aspic. To my daily vocabulary, I have added some colorful printing jargon such as "scanning," "stripping," and "trim size." And I have realized that when taking on such a project as this, one has to have a lot of help from others.

I was lucky. From the beginning, and all along the way, people have come to my assistance.

First, of course, there is Thelma. When I approached her originally with the idea of collecting her recipes for a cookbook, neither of us knew how many hours we would spend together, how many questions there would be to answer, how many phone calls would be made in the early morning and late at night. Through all of this, Thelma was her characteristic self: gracious, warm, and calm. I'd like to thank her for being such a wonderful partner, for all that I have learned about cooking, and for her sense of humor which manifests itself whenever I ask her if she is game for a sequel!

But to go back to the beginning, long before I ever met Thelma, I need to acknowledge my parents, both of whom are writers, for imparting their love of books to their children. I am indebted particularly to my father Robert K. Massie, a Pulitzer prize-winning biographer and a fine teacher of journalism, for all the hours he spent when I was a young girl reviewing and correcting my papers. This showed me that writing offers endless challenge and adventure.

And then there are those without whom this cookbook would never have come to fruition. If it hadn't been for our able baby sitters, Jean Campbell, Angela Miles, Krista Neal, Holly Young, and our surrogate grandmother/housekeeper Margie Warner, I would never have set foot out of our front door. I am grateful to all those with whom I spoke who shared information and reflections about Thelma. This helped me draw a much richer picture of her in my essay than I ever could have done by simply interviewing her. I would like to thank Mildred Buster and Mrs. C.V. Ethington for securing permission to reprint two recipes which Thelma has incorporated into her repertoire which come from that wonderful cookbook, *Bluegrass Winners*. Carolyn Batterton and Susan Shewmaker were invaluable to me as recipe testers and as enthusiastic supporters at every stage. I deeply appreciate their friendship and help. I was very lucky to have the assistance of three ladies at Shakertown, Brenda Roseman, Karen Preston, and Marsha Maddox. I would like to thank them for persistently and cheerfully coming to my assistance to clarify the mysteries of the copying and fax machines and for the countless favors they did for me. Don Pelly took the inviting photograph of Thelma in her kitchen on the cover, assisted by Kent Brown, and James Morris, and I am grateful to all three.

Larrie Curry is a fine illustrator and a generous friend, and Thelma and I are fortunate to have her work represented here as well as her assistance in the production of this book. It has been a special treat working with Gin Evans of Newburyport, Massachusetts on of the design of this book. I am grateful to her for her aesthetic sense, for the hearty laughs we have shared, and for every stomach ache she incurred while recipe testing because she could not resist overindulging in Thelma's treasures! My brother-in-law Sam Thomas has been supportive of this project from the first and knows more about putting books together than anyone I know. I deeply appreciate his encouragement, his skilled editing, and his assistance in the publishing of this book.

There are other reservoirs of talent in my family which I tapped. I would like to thank my stepfather Seymour Papert for his interest, his love, and for sharing his extensive knowledge about cooking. I am grateful to my sister Liz Massie and my brother Bob Massie, both good cooks and excellent writers, who read my manuscript and shared their thoughts in a most constructive manner. My mother Suzanne Massie Papert played a special role in the creation of *Thelma's Treasures*. She planted the seed for it by suggesting that I gather the recipes. She nurtured it along the way with her enthusiasm. A professional editor, she strengthened my essay with her excellent criticisms. For all of this, and for her devotion as a mother, I am very grateful.

As Thelma is a "seat of the pants" kind of cook, her recipes had to be tested for accuracy and clarification. I am fortunate to have the most zealous of kitchen assistants, my son, Ian, age two. He was always eager to don his apron, to mix and stir, to roll out and cut, to dip his small fingers into every bowl and lick every spoon, punctuating his efforts with such exclamations as "Mmmmmmmmmm," or "Good!" For his help and his unfailingly positive reinforcement, I am thankful.

But the one person who deserves the most special acknowledgment from all of us who know Thelma is my husband Jim. Without him, the secrets of Thelma's treasures probably would have followed her on to heaven. Jim wouldn't have that. He wanted generations to come to enjoy Thelma's good food and to remember her. He loved the idea of a cookbook from the first, and over the years he cheered (and sometimes prodded) me on. He gave me courage and made me happy by profusely complimenting all my efforts on paper and in the kitchen. He listened when necessary and guided when asked. He read and made invaluable suggestions both on the content and the appearance of the book. His aesthetic talent is reflected in the pages. For these gifts and for his love, I am forever thankful.

DECEMBER 1992

5

Contents

Introduction

The story of how this little cookbook came about begins four years ago, when my beau of the time, who became my husband, gave a large, catered dinner party in his house in honor of my thirtieth birthday. The meal was prepared and served by a diminutive elderly black woman, Mrs. Thelma Clay Linton, who lives in the small Central Kentucky town of Harrodsburg, some six miles from our farm.

One of the guests at the party was my mother. In addition to being a food connoisseur and an accomplished chef and hostess, she had worked during her long journalistic and writing career as an editor for the *Time-Life* cookbook series as well as put in a stint as managing editor at *Gourmet* magazine. A Swiss, she was raised with the European appreciation for and knowledge of good cooking, and over the years, her work has taken her around the world where she has gained a broad knowledge of many cuisines. At home, cooking is her hobby.

The food that night was pure and perfect Kentucky fare: fried chicken, light and crunchy on the outside, tender within; corn pudding, sweet and creamy; green beans, slightly smokey with a faint peppery flair. A sumptuous layer salad along with dinner rolls, remarkable in texture and taste, accompanied the meal. Strong, steaming coffee and tart lemon bars punctuated it. Mother, with all of her experience and her nose for a good dish, recognized Thelma's cooking for what it was—authentic, unpretentious, and utterly delicious.

"You should get these recipes," she suggested to me. "And if Thelma has any others, you should get those too."

I knew she was right. Thelma's recipes deserved and needed to be preserved. And, as she had no children to do this for her, nor had any Harrodsburg resident yet done so, it seemed to me that if Thelma were willing, I ought to take on the task. My husband Jim, a longtime admirer of Thelma and her cuisine, encouraged me to do so, and my brother-in-law, Sam, a writer and Kentucky historian, suggested that the recipes be gathered and published in a small book, an idea which was met with marked enthusiasm within our community.

When I approached Thelma with the proposal, I didn't know the challenges ahead. I didn't imagine how hard it would be to wrest time from her schedule and mine so that she could recreate from memory or retrieve from one of her many well-worn notebooks or cookbooks a certain speciality. As her list of treasured recipes is fairly concise, I thought incorrectly that typing it up and testing each dish could be done easily and quickly. Then, when Thelma and I got launched, I immediately noticed that the recipes for desserts outnumbered all other kinds of food. This suggested two things: that her appetizers and entrées were so good, that no one in town saw a need for change, and that Harrodsburg had a sweet tooth. I decided to maintain the imbalance to be true to Thelma's repertoire.

As I sat in her little kitchen, listening and scribbling, and months, even years passed, it became apparent to me that Thelma's greatest treasure was not, as some local folks might have guessed, the "receipt" for her rolls, although she did, after forty-five years of silence, divulge that secret. It was Thelma herself, a person of amazing talent and generous spirit who has quietly served and graced our community in myriad ways for over seven decades. During my time with her, I, as so many others have done so before me, fell in love with Thelma. Becoming her friend has been my greatest pleasure and reward in assembling this cookbook.

"The Best Cook in Harrodsburg"

In our town of Harrodsburg in Mercer County, Kentucky, Thelma Clay
Linton is an institution, revered for her outstanding country cuisine and
for her remarkable character. In these busy times when frequently both
spouses work and time is scarce, gracious dining at home is a rarity rather
than the rule. Yet, thanks to Thelma, Harrodsburg entertains and eats in a
style reminiscent of days gone by. Thelma is *the* person in town to call
when planning the food for any kind of social occasion: a Christmas party
or a Kentucky Derby gala, a wedding reception, or a women's club luncheon, a Fourth of July picnic, or an afternoon tea, a special dinner or an
evening of cocktails, all of which she prepares and serves for remarkably
reasonable fees. And she is always willing to fulfill single requests—a
birthday cake, a favorite pie, a batch of her famous rolls.

The night before Thanksgiving, Thelma holds vigil until dawn over suc-
cessive turkeys, roasting each one individually in her one small oven for
those folks who can't or won't roast their own, simply because she cooks the

moistest bird ever consumed. "I want the turkeys to be warm when the people come to pick them up," Thelma explains, laughing with incredulity at the thought of cooking some the day before and disclaiming any hardship on herself. "What it's hard on is my stove," she replies. "I burn my stoves up all the time." Over the years, she has lost count of all the replacements.

Acclaim for Thelma's country hams, rich and sophisticated in flavor, surpasses even that for her succulent turkeys. At most Harrodsburg parties, at any time of year, one of these delicacies can usually be found somewhere on the table if not in commanding entirety as a whole ham, then slivered and tucked between the layers of fresh biscuits. But come the holiday season, its presence is a surety. And, for many Harrodsburg residents, both former and current, Christmas Day is simply not complete without one. In the month of December, Thelma fills over a hundred orders for her hams, which, once cooked, she wraps in worn-out pillowcases or sheets and stacks in her kitchen and dining room until they are picked up or she can ship them to addresses across the country from the UPS collection point at the local cleaners.

And then there are her rolls, lighter than air, slightly sweet, hot and buttery. In Harrodsburg, when the words "Thelma's rolls" are spoken, people nod, purse their lips in speechless appreciation. For the uninitiated guest, their consumption marks a passage to a unique gastronomic haven. Until now, Thelma has guarded the secret of their creation. People beg for them, and she churns them out weekly by the dozens.

Such a schedule and such productivity at any age is impressive, but at eighty-three, it is extraordinary. Yet, her scarcely lined face and spry body defy her age. Standing just four feet eight inches tall, she's like a little sparrow, popping from branch to branch, continually busy, often in flight. "I am always in motion," Thelma admits with a smile. "Now ain't that somethin'?" She claims she is slowing down, but she still cleans house three days a week for three different families. ("I just never quit nobody," she says with an apologetic laugh.) She still presses a dress shirt to perfection for the bargain price of twenty-five cents. She still caters several parties a month, sometimes serving a handful, sometimes a hoard. And, she always has something on the stove or in the oven for somebody. "There's that man after his cake!," she's likely to jump up and exclaim when her doorbell rings. "That's a lady who likes to have lemon bars in her cookie jar," she'll mention after hanging up the telephone. "I'm boiling that chicken just to have some broth," she'll say as she points to the simmering pot on the burner. "People are always coming around to my doorstep asking, 'You got any broth?'"

When Thelma is asked to cook something or to cater a party, she writes down the customer's name, the date of delivery or service, and the requested item or menu on a slip of paper which she tapes to the kitchen cabinet door to the left of her sink. Often the notes on the cabinet overlap like scales on a fish, for Thelma is just not the type to turn people away. "Thelma will be head over heels with work, but she'll still say 'yes.' She doesn't know how to say 'no,'" Harrodsburg resident Ruth Ingram attests. "She's always there when I need her," Lib Culton of Harrodsburg admits, echoing the sentiments of all the hostesses in town. "She's the Rock of Gibraltar."

While Thelma sometimes marvels herself about the workload which "don't never seem to let up," she shrugs her shoulders about it all. "Sometimes I ask myself, now how can I fit all this in? But it always works out."

Thelma's success can be attributed to a wonderful blend of characteristics: experience, an unrelenting work ethic, and an extraordinary inner stability which has been strengthened over the years by a deep Christian faith. She approaches each day singly and with hope. "I let every day take care of itself," she says. "I always feel like everything is going to work out. I have enough faith to think that any problems can be solved."

And she applies such thinking in the kitchen. "Any time I go to cook anything, I say 'Lord, help this turn out!,'" Thelma admits with a laugh. "If I make a cake I say, 'Lord, help it to do all right, 'cause I don't have time to make another one!'"

But if by chance things do go awry, Thelma remains calm. "Nothing ruffles her," says David Shewmaker, who has known Thelma for years. Thelma recommends this stance for all serious cooks. "If you're going to be a good cook, you can't let yourself get upset," she cautions. "Getting upset don't help. Stay calm and have patience and just go along. You'll do a lot better. It's just natural with me to be that way. I don't like to rush. But I work fast," so fast that friends have warned her, she is "liable to run over herself one day."

"Thelma's personality is remarkable," Agnes Brown, a close friend of Thelma's and a fellow member of the Saint Peter's African Methodist Episcopal Church, attests. "She's just a real quiet, meek person. We can be working on a church dinner and while everybody else will be running around, Thelma will be busy working. She don't have too much to say, she just goes about her way."

In Harrodsburg, Thelma can often be seen going about her way in her gray 1986 Buick Century, her small face, framed by a little cloche hat, barely visible as she peeps over the wheel. Step into the post office and she is sending off her electricity bill or a donation to some charity. Shop at the grocery store and she's scrutinizing the vegetables in the produce aisle, her cart loaded with ingredients for the next party she is catering.

Wherever Thelma goes, people in town are glad to see her. "It's all I can do to run up to her and hug the dickens out of her when I see her at the grocery store," Dan Kidd, former director of the Harrodsburg Chamber of Commerce admits. "She is here every day," Lonnie Campbell one of the owners of the local Gateway Market confirms. "Everybody knows her. Everybody likes her. She's a willing, kind, and very giving person." "People delight in being around Thelma," states Carolyn Royalty, the county extension agent for home economics, who oversees the Harrod Home-makers, a group in which Thelma has participated for decades.

Despite Thelma's many responsibilities and engagements, she always seems to find time for others. She visits elderly relatives and friends (some of them younger than she) not only in Harrodsburg but as far away as Lexington and Louisville, and sometimes in outlying states. Often she acts as a liaison between the black and white communities in town. When people give her clothing or toys that children or grandchildren have outgrown, Thelma finds a happy recipient. "She looks after a lot of people," Jane Hatchett of Harrodsburg asserts. "She takes a lot of pleasure in helping others."

Help was certainly what local resident, Nancy Gabhart, needed several Christmases ago when she and her family found themselves without the *pièce de résistance* for their holiday meal. "I had asked Thelma to fix us a turkey for Christmas," Mrs. Gabhart recalls. "When the time came, I bought a turkey and gave it to my husband to deliver. Christmas Day arrived, and I never heard from Thelma, so I called her and said, 'Thelma, where's the turkey?' and she said, 'What turkey?'"

Thelma explained that when no turkey appeared, she presumed a change of menu had occurred. The two ladies then deduced that Mr. Gabhart had mistakenly given the turkey to Anna Laura Pittman, who had made bourbon balls in the past for the Gabharts, and who was all too pleased to receive such a fine bird. "I hung up the phone and started thinking about all the places I could beg, borrow or steal a turkey," Mrs. Gabhart recounts. "Then Thelma called. 'I think it's a shame that you are not going to have any Christmas dinner,' she said. 'I have talked to Anna Laura Pittman and she has half of the turkey left after her Christmas dinner last night which she will give to you. And I'll make you gravy and dressing and anything else you want me to fix.'"

Over the years, such thoughtful acts have won Thelma many friends and admirers who trust her completely and who often ask unusual favors of her which she obligingly fulfills. Mrs. Hatchett recalls that once when she was vacationing in Florida, it occurred to her that she needed to turn in a certificate of deposit to her hometown bank. "I called Thelma and told her where the key to the bank box was in our house. She went down to the First Federal, cashed the CD and deposited the money."

On another occasion, when Harrodsburg resident Bea Devine went away on her vacation, the family silver was left with Thelma for safekeeping. When Hattie Barnet who had moved from Harrodsburg to Florida wanted an American flag placed on her husband's grave in the town's Springhill Cemetery, she sent a note and money to Thelma. When Hall Willis' son died, he called Thelma and said, "You take care of things. "You know how to do this." Thelma made all of the funeral arrangements.

"Even when I was a little girl," Thelma reminisces and laughs, "people used to say 'Thelma Clay can do it!,' no matter what it was." Her ability to master whatever she takes on coupled with her now legendary prowess in the kitchen are the obvious reasons for her success as a caterer. This combination puts every host and hostess at ease, and all who have engaged Thelma would agree with the words of Mrs. Culton: "When Thelma walks into my kitchen and I walk out, I feel so comfortable. I just know that everything will be done and that my guests will be well taken care of." But two other qualities as essential as her confidence and experience include her financial acumen, and her extraordinary diplomacy.

This latter talent was recognized by the Mercer County Extension Homemaker Council, representing seventeen different clubs and 320 members which, in 1973, elected her vice-president. The next year she ascended to the presidency. When her term ended in 1976, the predominantly white membership reelected her president. "She is the only black county homemaker president Mercer County has ever had," says Mrs.

Royalty. "She conducts a really good business meeting with excellent parliamentary procedure. Although she is soft-spoken, she commands great respect as a leader." She subsequently was honored with a life-time in membership to her local club, the Harrod Homemakers, in appreciation for her service.

In 1979, the Fort Harrod Business and Professional Women's Club showed their respect for Thelma by presenting her with the "Woman of the Year" award in recognition of her professionalism, business savvy, and devotion to family and religious values. "Thelma has an array of excellent qualities that all of us should emulate," says member Elaine Wooldridge. "We wanted to honor her for her many talents and contributions to our community and for all that she had done for our group over the years."

Although Thelma has given of herself to many, the primary recipient of her talent, good will, and effort has always been St. Peter's African Methodist Episcopal Church. Since 1927 when she joined, she has been one the most active and faithful members—"the ring leader,"—as congregation member Mrs. Brown describes her. Her pastor, Reverend J.T. Ballew calls her "a missionary in every sense of the word. "She gives and goes out for people regardless of who they are," says he. "She cooks for those that have and those that don't. She's cooked for those who couldn't pay. She feeds the hungry. She'll help anybody, it doesn't matter what color they are or what their social status is. If they are human beings, she will reach out. She's loved by everybody within the church. People look up to Thelma and admire her. If there is such a things as a role model for a Christian, she is it."

No one seems to have an accurate record of all the offices Thelma has held at Saint Peter's over the years, nor of how long she has fulfilled them. Thelma herself can't remember how long she has been the church steward, keeping the financial records of the pastor's salary and expenses, as well as all of the donations made to charities, and attending quarterly conferences. For years she has also been a church stewardess in charge of the altar, the preparation of the communal table, and the baptismal font. She is the current president of the Missionary Society, a group which organizes and provides aid for the needy and the sick. The plaque on her dining room wall commemorates her nineteen years as church secretary. And, even in church, Thelma cannot stay out of the kitchen. Whenever there is a church dinner or picnic, Thelma is definitely a contributor if not the organizer and primary cook. Every presiding pastor has benefitted from her generosity and the gift of her time.

Today, when Mr. Ballew goes on retreats or to church conferences, Thelma is one of the delegation. "If she is not cooking!," he comments with a chuckle, "then, we're on the road—to missionary meetings, to our annual conference, our district conference, our Sunday School convention or planning meetings."

With all of these obligations and her missionary work, it is sometimes hard to find Thelma at home. But ring the doorbell of her small white house with the green roof and chimneys on North Main Street and if she's there, she'll come presently to the door wearing a splattered apron or an old workdress. "Why, hello there!," she'll say with her warm grin revealing her two dimples and the little gap between her front teeth. "Come on in!"

Her shot-gun house, one room wide and four rooms deep, is old-fashioned and homey, with a mixture of furniture dating from the turn of the last century to the middle of this one and an eclectic decor of Victorian bric-à-brac, gilded porcelain, crotcheted pillows, brass lamps, and religious art. Photographs of family and friends—parents, siblings, nieces, cousins, godchildren—hang on the walls, are clustered on the mantels and tables. There is her father Beverly Clay as a young man in the early 1900s dressed in a high collared shirt and suit. He is sitting tall, his hands resting on his lap, his dark eyes staring out of the frame with a proud yet vulnerable gaze. There is her mother Nannie Brown Clay in a pressed, pleated blouse, floor length skirt, hair parted in the middle sweeping from her temples into a bun. She is smiling sweetly as she stands in front of her white clapboard house with her husband and two girls in white pinafores and black bows, four-year old Eliza Jane, and Thelma Lee, age six.

"I've got something in the oven!," Thelma is likely to explain at this point as she excuses herself, although no announcement is necessary as delicious aromas from the kitchen *always* greet you in the front room.

The scent will intensify as you follow her through the living room into a bedroom with a grand four-poster bed and two workhorse thirty-year-old televisions stacked one upon the other topped by an old RCA radio. You will pass the bookcase harboring such titles as *A Daily Guide to Miracles* by Oral Roberts; *Philosophers of English Literature*; *The Simple Spirit, The Family Book of Best Loved Poems*; Rudyard Kipling's: *A Selection of His Stories Old and New*; three dictionaries, two *Bibles*, and four copies of the *African Methodist Episcopal Church Discipline* of disparate years. On a table nearby, the daily *Lexington Herald Leader* lies open beside another Bible and a small stack of cookbooks which Thelma is reading for pleasure.

Continue through the dining room where silver platters, serving bowls, coffee pots and pitchers on the side board and in glass cabinets gleam through their protective plastic bags, and you come to the kitchen, that small room with the sloping floor and the 1950's fixtures—the heart of the house.

There, Thelma is opening the oven, peeping in at a batch of rolls. The warm, sweet smell of fresh bread fills the air. A cake ready for icing waits on the counter; a chocolate pie, its peaks of whirled meringue perfectly singed a tawny brown sits on the kitchen table. In the sink two lacy aprons worn at a party the night before soak in a yellow plastic bucket filled with sudsy water. The washing machine in the adjoining utility room churns heartily. A perfectly pressed white uniform hangs on the door. The old electric clock above the refrigerator says 10:00.

"Oh, I got up at 5:00 this morning," Thelma replies when asked how she has had time to do all this. And then she might add "I still got more, too. There's a death in town, so I am cookin' up a storm. They'll just cook you to death when there's a funeral!" Or she might explain "I'm doin' a luncheon for the women's club." Or perhaps, although it is rare, she'll say that she is cooking for herself, trying out a new dish before she offers it to anyone else, or treating herself to some gingerbread, a dessert which she bakes for herself about once a year "when she takes the notion."

Ask her for the recipe of these creations, and she stops to ponder. "Now where did I find that?" she'll wonder for she has over a hundred cookbooks. The difficulty of recollection is further compounded by the fact that Thelma frequently deviates from the text, adding and deleting ingredients as her mood and supplies dictate, contributing her own special flavors and flair, so that she has to recall her modifications as well.

Nevertheless, there are some likely sources, such as *Southern Living's* annual cookbook series which she purchased during the late '70s and the '80s. "I don't use many of them," she admits about the series, "but 1979 seems to fall my way all the time." Other favorites include *Vintage Vicksburg, The Springfield Women's Club Tasting Tour of Washington City,* and *Bluegrass Winners.*

If not in these places, Thelma will check the "raggedy book," her primary trove of culinary delights garnered over the decades. The orange spiral notebook is jammed with newspaper clippings, index cards and handwritten recipes on pages now yellowed, tattered, and streaked with ingredients of cooking days past. When not in use, the raggedy book is wrapped up in a plastic grocery sack secured by a rubber band and stuffed in a sagging kitchen drawer with other cookbooks of all dimensions in similar states of disintegration.

"It's terrible," Thelma says with a resigned shrug about her cookbook collection. "I tear them up so bad. But there's just no more room. I've got a bookshelf out in the utility room but look at it!" She throws open the doors of a cabinet in the next room, revealing dozens of books, hard, spiral, and paper bound, many with rubber bands around them to keep the covers from dropping off. "I'm goin' to put some in the shed. The ones I don't use too much." But as if foreseeing the difficulties of banishing any to an out building, she adds shaking her head, "Cookbooks just fascinate me. I can't hardly turn one out. I say I am not going to buy any more, and then I see something that interests me and I say 'here I go again!'"

There was a time when Thelma didn't use any cookbooks, a time, indeed, when she knew nothing about cooking at all. Yet from her earliest days she had an appreciative palate, thanks to her versatile mother. "She done anything," Thelma recalls. "She done like I do. She washed, she cleaned and she cooked for other people." Out of Nannie Clay's kitchen came remarkable culinary creations: chicken and dumplings, apple pies, and "big, fluffy white cakes, stacked three stories high." Children, however, were not allowed to cross the threshold to observe how these specialities were made.

Born on the twenty-first of July, 1909, in Mackville, in Washington County, Kentucky, Thelma is the only one of the three Clay children to survive to adulthood. Her brother, Rastus died in infancy, her sister, Eliza, in adolescence. She also lost her father, who "hauled, cropped, drove horses, and did everything," when she was only nine years old. Two years later, Thelma's mother remarried and moved the family to Perryville to live with her new husband, Ira Sleet. Anxious to make a little money, Thelma went to work shortly thereafter as a resident baby-sitter for the only child of the town undertaker Arthur Coyle and his wife. Thelma never moved back home again. She was twelve years old.

Madelaine Coyle was a good cook, and for the first two years in her employ, Thelma quietly studied her actions in the kitchen. Then, one morning, Thelma decided to surprise the family. She slipped into the kitchen, lit the stove and cooked a sumptuous breakfast of bacon, eggs, toast, white gravy, and coffee. Drawn to the kitchen at the usual hour Mrs. Coyle was amazed and delighted by the delectable mixture of hot smells which greeted her. "Why, Thelma?," she exclaimed, "you can *cook!*," and thus said, hung up her apron—permanently.

"I got started and she quit," Thelma recalls with a chuckle. "I didn't use cookbooks then. I just picked it up and went."

Thelma also picked up and went several years later when the Coyles decided to move from Perryville to Harrodsburg, leaving her family and school ten miles behind. That might have been the end of Thelma's education, as Harrodsburg at that time had no school for blacks. However, rather than abandon her studies which she enjoyed (particularly mathematics), Thelma found daily transportation to Danville, five miles away, where she attended the Bates High School. A model student, she graduated in May, 1927.

Four months later, on September third, Thelma married Sterling Linton, a young man whom she had met two years before while strolling down the streets of Harrodsburg one afternoon with a friend. They were happily married fifty-two years until Sterling's death at the age of seventy-three in 1979. They had no children. When asked why, Thelma explains quietly, "it just never did happen." Then her voice brightens as she adds "so we raised up other people's."

Although Thelma is discreet about her late husband's qualities, it seems from those who knew him that he lived up to his name. According to my husband, Jim Thomas, president of Shakertown at Pleasant Hill where Sterling worked for seventeen years as a maintenance employee, he shared his wife's remarkable work ethic. "Sterling did his work with great élan and perfection," Jim recalls. "He was superb working outside, digging holes for fence posts, cutting grass, planting trees. The harder the job, the better he liked it. He was an extremely gifted gardener. He could grow the most beautiful vegetables that had wonderful visual appeal and were delicious to eat. He loved flowers, and in his care they flourished.

"Sterling was one of the most gentle people I have ever known," Jim continues. "He had a wonderful, warm way with animals. Dogs were crazy about him. There was a special canine in Sterling's life, a little stray curdog called Winnie, that's short for Winter Shaker. (Winter Shakers came at the first frost and left after spring plowing.) But Winnie soon developed the good sense to stay at Shakertown for she was loved by all—staff, friends, visitors. But the person that she considered her master and whom she adored above all was Sterling. She seemed to know exactly the days he would be working, and on those days she would wait in the parking area for him to come. When he drove up, she would charge the car. Sterling—a bear of a man, not particularly tall, but very stoutly built and with huge, strong arms—would gather Winnie up in a warm embrace. That's how he started every day at Shakertown."

Sterling's comfortably burly figure was a tribute to his wife's talents, and Thelma doesn't deny the fact that he appreciated her cooking. "He liked to eat," Thelma recalls. Meat and bread and gravy," followed by one her pies or cakes or a batch of her cookies. Every summer, he would bring the bounty of his prolific vegetable gardens into Thelma's kitchen and ask her to can. "There were bushels and bushels," Thelma remembers. "I used to say, Summers are no pleasure."

In 1931, Thelma and Sterling moved into the little house on North Main Street where she still lives. As the Coyles had moved back to Perryville, Thelma went to work for Lawrence and Verna Walker, Mrs. Coyle's stepfather and mother who owned a garage in town. Seven days a week, Thelma cooked, cleaned, and ironed for the Walker family. When the grandchildren visited, which was regularly, she baby-sat. "I done it all," she remembers. "But I didn't have to work all day Sunday. I'd go in the morning and cook their dinner and then get home in time to go to church."

After Mrs. Walker's children were grown and her husband had died, the workload in her home lessened. So Thelma took on additional jobs as the the weekly housekeeper for several other families in Harrodsburg. Mrs. Walker's death in 1970 ended their forty year association.

Although Thelma already had plenty to do, she decided at that time to start a small catering business. She had cooked so many meals over the years and had often helped to prepare dinners at her church that she had a roster of people who regularly requested her specialities. Her business began slowly, but once launched grew steadily, so much so that by 1977, when a food writer from the *Los Angeles Times* who was visiting Shaker-town heard of Thelma's reputation, she insisted on interviewing her for a story. "Her name pops up automatically, like a jackpot, when the subject is cooking," the article begins. The author then explains that every time she asked who in the area made the best rolls, the best corn pudding, the best cakes, indeed, who was *the best cook in the county*, the answer was always the same: Mrs. Thelma Linton. That article, Thelma recalls with obvious pride and delight, stirred a momentary flurry of national fan mail addressed exclusively in such unorthodox ways as: "To Thelma Linton,

The Best Cook in Harrodsburg" or "To Mrs. Sterling Linton, Harrodsburg, Kentucky. Please find her!"

Of course, the mail carrier knew exactly where to deliver the letters. "Everybody knows Mrs. Linton and her cooking," John Peavler, front desk clerk at the Harrodsburg Post Office asserts. "I remember once when a lady who was visiting in town came in. She wanted to know the street address of 'the lady on North Main who made the rolls.' Naturally, I knew who she was talking about. But, even if she hadn't mentioned the street, I would have sent her to Mrs. Linton, knowing her reputation for fine cooking."

Mr. Peavler reflects for a moment on Thelma's cuisine, especially her butterscotch pie, the delectable memory of which causes him to shake his head slowly from side to side and whistle appreciatively. "I used to live a few houses up from Mrs. Linton. You should see the street around Easter, Thanksgiving, and Christmas! Cars are lined up in front of her house, and people one after the other are coming and going picking up holiday dishes!"

When Thelma began her business she had no inkling that such success would follow. "It started small," she recalls, "and it just kept getting bigger and bigger!" Today she caters twenty-five to thirty parties a year and sometimes more. She's been known to do weddings for 600 guests. During the holiday season, one has to book her two to three months in advance. Her telephone rings regularly with callers requesting her specialties. Few days go by without someone knocking on her door to see what she might have for sale in her refrigerator, or to discuss plans for an upcoming social event.

When Thelma caters a party, she arrives early, the cavernous trunk of her old Buick stocked with boxes, pots, and chafing dishes. She's wearing a white uniform. Her hair, graying on the sides, is pulled back and tucked neatly into a hair net. Her shoes are sensible, solid, flat. In the kitchen, she sets out the sauce pans and utensils she will need, turns on the oven, makes the coffee, artistically arranges the appetizers on platters, readies the table.

As the party begins and she appears on the threshold with a platter of spicy cheese wafers or sausage balls, rich asparagus rolls or chicken livers wrapped in bacon, guests discretely jockey for position vis-à-vis the plate while still trying to follow the train of conversation. Fortunately, Thelma moves gracefully through the crowd, quickly accommodating all.

Later, when the chafing dishes filled with roast turkey or country ham, corn pudding, or green beans on the dining room table begin to empty, Thelma slips in from the kitchen with a steaming replenishment. When the time comes, coffee and some kind of delectable dessert are ready on the sideboard.

As the evening comes to a close and the last guests are slipping away, Thelma is at the kitchen sink, finishing up the dishes. The china and the silver are back in place. The leftovers are tucked in the refrigerator. The counters are clean.

She looks a little tired as she makes out a bill in a notebook and tears out a sheet, but she's smiling. She is glad the party was a success, that's why she cooks, she says, to make people happy. "When I fix something and it pleases people, it makes me feel real good," she confesses.

Perhaps, this is the secret of her longevity and youthfulness, the compensations she has earned through a lifetime of contribution. She has found truth in the Christian maxim that it is better to give than to receive. In providing for others, she creates her own joy.

Thelma justifiably could boast of all of her accomplishments and good works, yet no one is more modest and humble than she. Unimpressed with compliments, she is content to satisfy. She knows who she is and what she does well. She has achieved a deep and unchallengeable harmony within herself which manifests itself in her unshakable serenity and in an aura of dignity which surrounds her. She has a quiet and kind sense of humor about life and human beings, including herself. She has lived long and seen much, and addresses suffering with graciousness. In her company, people feel at home.

In Harrodsburg, we all know that when Thelma finally leaves us, an era will have ended. She is, as my husband Jim says, "a legend, south of the Kentucky River. When she stops catering, an old-fashioned way of gracious dinning will be gone from this area forever." Others in town repeat the words of Mrs. Ingram who once expressed that "when something happens to Thelma, "we will all have to quit entertaining!" "She's a jewel," says Reverend Ballew, "and there aren't too many like her, either." "She's such a dream person," Mr. Campbell of the Gateway Market agrees. "I don't guess there's a better person going than her, really."

So far, fortunately for all of us, Thelma keeps going, working every day, with few signs of hanging up the towel. Although she might entertain thoughts of retirement, she says at present she just can't "find her way out." And she still just won't say 'No.'

It's a good thing, for if she had known the word, she might not have relinquished her culinary secrets, most especially the recipe for her incomparable rolls.

When asked why, after all, she decided to share the treasures in her trove Thelma pauses and smiles before explaining. "I decided to do this cookbook because I was getting old. When I was younger I wouldn't have given out my recipes. But I figured that by the time this book came out, I'd be ready to quit."

Let us hope, lest this little book do us all a disservice, that she is not serious.

Appetizers

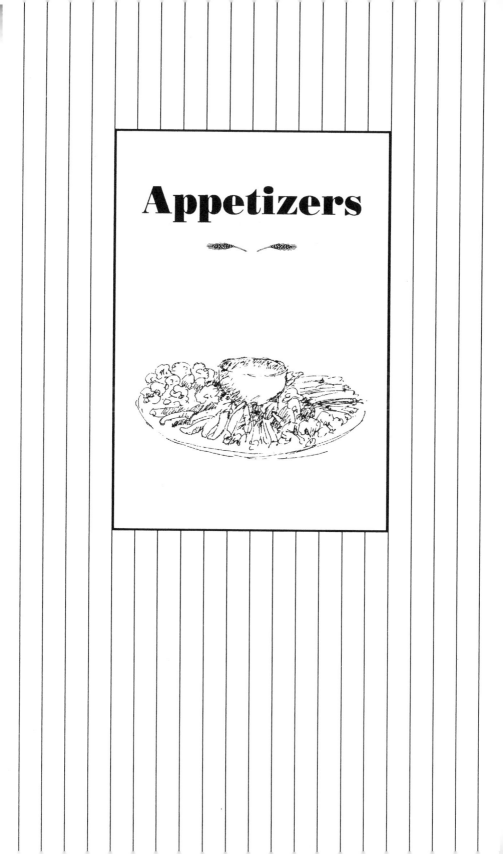

Asparagus Rolls

"Every time I do a party, they want asparagus rolls.
They're just different than anything that's been around,
I guess....This recipe is hard, though. There are too
many steps. Rolling that bread wears you out."

1 loaf white sandwich bread
1 egg
1 (8 ounce) package cream cheese
1 (4 ounce) package blue cheese
1 to 1-1/2 cans asparagus
melted butter, at least 2 sticks

Cut off the crusts of the bread and roll each slice really thin.

Beat up the egg until stiff. Mix it up with the cream cheese and the blue cheese real good. Spread some on each slice of bread, then lay one asparagus on top. Roll up the slices like jelly rolls.

Roll each one in melted butter. Place seam side down on a baking sheet. Freeze at least for an hour. (They can be frozen indefinitely until use.) Defrost slightly. Cut into three bite-size pieces. Bake at 400° for 12 to 15 minutes until the rolls begin to brown.

Makes roughly 25 rolls.

Cheese Straws

*"After you fix these, keep them in the refrigerator.
They stay real crisp for about a week."*

10 ounces Cracker Barrel Cheddar cheese, grated
1 teaspoon cayenne pepper
l teaspoon salt
1 stick (8 tablespoons) butter
1-1/2 cups flour

Preheat the oven to 350°. Work all of the ingredients together by hand.
Roll out like biscuit dough. Cut into strips with a pastry cutter or a knife.
Get a regular cookie sheet and don't grease it. Cook for about 8 to 10
minutes. Feel the sticks with your finger, they should feel kind of hard.
Don't get them brown.

Makes about five to six dozen.

Cheese Wafers

"Mr. Cogar used to make these. He had pretty little crinkles in his! These freeze well. This makes five to six dozen."

1 stick (8 tablespoons) butter
4 ounces Cracker Barrel Cheddar cheese, grated
1 cup Rice Krispies
1 cup flour
red pepper to taste

Mix the butter and the cheese together by hand. Add all of the other ingredients. Pinch the dough off into little balls. Dip a fork in cold water and flatten each ball.

Bake at 375° for 17 minutes or until golden brown.

Chicken Livers Wrapped in Bacon

"A mess to fool with, but real good."

1 pound chicken livers
1/4 cup brown sugar
2 tablespoons Worcestershire sauce
3-4 tablespoons soy sauce
bacon slices

Wash the chicken livers in a sieve and drain them well. Mix up the brown sugar, Worcestershire and soy sauces in a large bowl and add the chicken livers. Turn them so they get coated with the juices. Cover the bowl and let sit overnight.

Wrap each chicken liver with half a slice of bacon and secure it with a toothpick. Bake at 450° for about 20 minutes until the bacon is brown.

Shrimp Mold

2 pounds fresh shrimp, small or medium
2 (8 ounce) packages cream cheese
2-2/3 cups thick tomato soup
2 tablespoons gelatin
1/2 cup cold water
1/2 cup finely grated onion

1 cup finely chopped celery
a few dashes of Tabasco
2 cups mayonnaise

Peel, devein and rinse the shrimp. Throw them in a pot of boiling water and cook for 10 minutes. Drain and run cold water over them to stop them from cooking. Chop them up. In another bowl beat the cream cheese until it is smooth. In a saucepan, heat the tomato soup. Dissolve the gelatin in the cold water and add to the soup. Stir until the soup is smooth. Add the soup-gelatin mixture to the cream cheese. Mix in everything else but the mayonnaise. When it is all mixed up well, fold in the mayonnaise. Pour into an unoiled fish mold and chill. When it comes time to unmold it, run a wet, warm cloth over the bottom several times and turn the mold over on a platter. Serve with crackers.

Spinach Balls

2 (10 ounce) packages frozen chopped spinach
2 cups herb seasoning stuffing mix
1 cup Parmesan cheese
6 eggs, beaten

3/4 cup margarine, softened
salt, pepper

Cook the spinach and drain. Then combine it with all of the other ingredients in a bowl and mix well. Roll into balls. Place on a baking sheet and freeze them. When frozen, place in an airtight plastic bag until you plan to use them.

When you are ready to cook them, place the frozen balls on a lightly greased baking sheet and bake at 350° for 10 minutes or until lightly browned.

Makes 50-70 balls.

Sausage Balls

"Mix the cheese and the sausage together first. It seems like it does better. It doesn't take as much working to get everything mixed up and moist. People think you can do this in a few minutes but you can't. They do finally work up now, just keep working."

1 pound hot sausage
1/2 pound mild sausage
6 ounces grated sharp Cheddar cheese
6 cups Bisquick

Mix up all of the ingredients. Form into balls. (These can keep indefinitely in the freezer.) Bake at 350° until brown, approximately half an hour. Makes 75-100 balls.

Vegetable Dip

"This will keep a week."

1 (8 ounce) package cream cheese
4 ounces blue cheese
1/3 cup mayonnaise
few drops of Worcestershire sauce
1 tablespoon dried onion flakes
few drops Tobasco sauce

Combine the cream cheese, blue cheese and the mayonnaise. Mix well. Add the rest of the ingredients. If the dip needs thinning, use more mayonnaise. Put it in the mixer and beat it up real good. Serve with vegetables.

Spinach Dip

"Make this a day ahead of time."

2 (10 ounce) packages chopped cooked spinach, well drained
2 cups sour cream
1 cup mayonnaise
1 cup freshly minced parsley
1 cup chopped scallion tops
1 teaspoon Beau Monde seasoning
1 teaspoon dill weed
salt, pepper

Blend all of the ingredients together, season to taste, and refrigerate. Serve with vegetables.

Derby Menu

Ham Biscuits

Turkey Sandwiches with Dressing

Asparagus Rolls

Sausage Balls

Spinach Dip

Vegetable Dip

Chicken Livers Wrapped in Bacon

Cheese Straws

Strawberries in Powdered Sugar

Lemon Bars

Double Chocolate Cookies

Crème de Menthe Bars

Pimiento Cheese

"You can buy this at the store, but people say they like mine better. Most anything you make at home is better than what you buy."

1 pound Cheddar cheese
1 pound Velveeta cheese
1 small jar pimientos, undrained
1 tablespoon onion, grated
1/4 teaspoon garlic powder
1/4 teaspoon MSG (optional)
1 dash cayenne pepper
1 cup mayonnaise

Put all of the ingredients in the mixer and beat them up. Serve with crackers or make a ribbon sandwich with three slices of bread and one layer of pimiento cheese and one layer of Benedictine (see recipe on page 33).

Benedictine

*"I've been making this a long time. What you buy
in the store is so thin that I started making my own.
People like the combination of Benedictine and
pimiento cheese."*

2 (8 ounce) packages cream cheese, softened
1 large cucumber, peeled and minced
1 medium onion, minced
1 teaspoon mayonnaise
1/4 teaspoon salt
2 or 3 drops green food coloring

Beat the cheese in the mixer. Blend in the other ingredients well and chill.
When ready to serve, spread on sliced bread.

Shower Menu

Pimiento and Benedictine Sandwiches
Chicken Salad Party Shells
Fruit Bowl
Crème de Menthe Bars

Party Shells

"You can put anything that you want in the party shells. You can make little lemon pies, little chocolate tarts. Fill them with anything. Fill them with chicken salad. When you make them use one small egg, and I mean a <u>small</u> egg, 'cause if you use a large egg, they won't turn out."

1 small egg
1 cup and 2 tablespoons flour
1 stick (8 tablespoons) margarine
1/4 teaspoon salt

Make the dough the day before using them (You could make it up to three days before.) Beat your egg first. Then mix it and all of the other ingredients together and chill. When you are ready to use them, take the dough out of the refrigerator and pinch off little balls to press into the little ungreased pastry shells. Bake at 400° for 10 to 12 minutes.

Makes on average 36 or 37 shells.

Sausage Casserole

"Several years ago, a lady who had been a guest of Mrs. Phyllis Campbell's once called me up and said she wanted to hold a party and serve this casserole. So I called Mrs. Campbell up and asked her for the recipe, and she was nice to give it out. I've made it a lot since then. Everybody likes it and it's real good for a brunch. Make it the day before because it's not the easiest thing in the world to do. There are a lot of steps."

12 eggs, beaten and scrambled
3 tablespoons butter
1 pound sausage
1/4 cup onions, chopped
2 ounces sliced mushrooms

Melt the butter and scramble your eggs. In a different pan, cook your sausage until crumbly and brown. Remove it from the pan and sauté the onions in the drippings. Mix all of the ingredients together and put in a casserole dish. Make your sauce.

Sauce:
    2 tablespoons butter
    2-1/2 tablespoons flour
    2 cups milk
    1/2 teaspoon salt
    1/2 teaspoon pepper
    4 ounces American cheese
    4 tablespoons butter
    2 cups whole wheat bread crumbs
    dash of paprika

Melt the butter in a saucepan, then add the flour. Cook for a minute or two before adding the milk, seasonings and cheese. Cook until thickened. Pour on top of the casserole. Top the casserole with the butter cut in pieces, the fresh whole wheat bread crumbs, and a pinch of paprika. At this point if you want, you can put the casserole in the refrigerator and let it sit overnight.

When you are ready to eat it, put the casserole in an oven preheated to 350° and cook it until the casserole bubbles up real good.

Meats

Baked Country Ham

*"I don't remember when I started cookin' country hams. I used
to cook them on top of the stove, but they are heavy and that's
too much lifting. When people used to kill hogs, they'd put the
lard in a big tin can and that's what you'd cook your ham in,
either that or a big kettle on top of the stove. Now I cook my
hams in an electric roaster that sits on the floor in the utility
room. You can do them in the oven just the same, but it's
so hard on my stove, so I quit. 'Course if I get run over,
I'll cook some in the oven."*

1 country ham (approximately 15 pounds)
water
1 cup vinegar
2 cups brown sugar
2 tablespoons pickling spice

Topping:
    1/2 cup cracker crumbs
    1/2 cup brown sugar
    dash of ground cloves

Put the ham in to soak overnight in plenty of water and a cup of vinegar. If the ham is real salty, soak it longer than that. When the ham has been soaked, take it out of the water and scrub it real good. Preheat the oven to 350°. Put the ham in a roasting pan that has a cover. Put in about two cups of brown sugar and about two tablespoons of pickling spice. Pour in enough water to cover the ham. Put the top on the roasting pan. Cook the ham in the oven for two hours on one side. Then turn it over and cook for two hours on the other. Turn off the oven and leave the roasting pan in until the oven is cool. Then take the ham out. The bone should slip right out. Take the skin off.

Mix up the cracker crumbs, the brown sugar and the ground cloves. Put this on top of the ham and put the ham back in the oven at 400° and let the crust brown.

Remove the ham from the oven and tie it up in a cloth. Anything that is big enough is all right. Let the ham get cold before you slice it.

Ham Biscuits

homemade biscuits (see recipe page 54)
sliced country ham
butter

Moisten the ham with melted butter and lay it on the biscuits.

Ham Slices and Red Eye Gravy

Place a 1/4" ham slice with a 1/4 cup of water in a skillet. Bring to a boil, cover and cook until the water has been absorbed. Sprinkle with brown sugar to taste and let brown on both sides. Remove ham and add 1/2 cup of water. Heat through, stirring to scrape up brown bits in the pan.

Ham Croquettes

"You can use your ham scraps to make these. They can be prepared ahead of time and frozen. If you do this, wait until you're ready to use them before frying them. I always use fresh bread crumbs."

1 cup ground ham scraps
1 cup white sauce (recipe follows)
1/2 teaspoon Worcestershire sauce
1/2 teaspoon dry mustard
1 egg, beaten
toasted bread crumbs

To each cup of ham, add one cup of thick white sauce, a half teaspoon of Worcestershire sauce, a half teaspoon of dry mustard, and one egg. Add enough toasted bread crumbs to mold this mixture into croquettes. Roll the croquettes in more crumbs for coating. Fry in deep fat until brown. Serve with white sauce or cheese sauce.

White Sauce / Cheese Sauce

1 stick (8 tablespoons) butter
2 tablespoons flour
1 cup milk
6 slices Velveeta (optional)

Melt your butter in a saucepan over medium heat. Stir in the flour. Pour in the milk and cook, stirring, until it gets thick. It don't take but a few minutes. If you want to make a cheese sauce put six slices of Velveeta into the thickened sauce and don't let the sauce cook much or it will separate. This makes approximately two cups.

Roast Turkey

"Keep this recipe to yourself because people are going to think this is wild....I can't tell you exactly when the turkey is done. I can smell myself when it is ready, but I don't know if anyone else can do that or not. It just smells like it is ready to eat. It has that 'done' smell."

1 turkey (13 to 15 pounds)
salt
pepper
2 sticks (1 cup) butter
water

Soak the turkey in a handful of salt and water overnight while it thaws. The next day wash the turkey real good inside and out.

Put the turkey on a piece of Reynolds Wrap and add a little more salt inside and out. Sprinkle pepper over that.

Melt a stick of butter and pour it all over the turkey. Melt another stick of butter and soak it up with a rag. Spread the buttered cloth over the turkey, breast-side up.

Wrap the turkey up real good in the Reynolds Wrap. Cover it with a paper sack on top of that. Put the turkey in a roaster and pour a cup full of water into the pan. Then put the cover on. Cook the turkey at 325° in a preheated oven three to five hours, depending on the size. A 13-15 pound turkey will take about four hours. It takes a full hour just to start cooking.

Turkey Gravy

Remove the turkey from the roasting pan. Scrape up the brown pieces and mix with the broth in the pan. Then pour about one cup of the liquid into a saucepan. This will make about one quart of gravy. Let the broth come to a boil. In the meantime, in a bowl mix about three tablespoons of flour with a little water and make a paste. Then add two cups of water to the paste and stir it well. Add this to the broth. Let it all cook until thick, stirring constantly.

Season if necessary, but the broth should have enough flavor on its own.

Turkey Dressing

*"Nobody's going to go to the trouble to make homemade biscuits
and homemade corn bread, but that's what I do."*

homemade biscuits, homemade corn bread both in equal portions
a little Pepperidge Farm herb stuffing
celery, chopped
onion, chopped
turkey broth

Break up the biscuits and the corn bread and mix with the stuffing and as
much celery and onion you want. Dilute some of the turkey broth from
the pan. (You can also use chicken broth that you have on hand.) Add it
to the dressing mixture. Form the dressing into balls. Bake at 350° for half
an hour.

Turkey Sandwiches

white and whole wheat bread (I use Evergreen Bread)
mayonnaise
Dijon mustard
turkey slices

Cut off the crusts of the bread. Mix up the mayonnaise and the mustard
in equal parts. Spread on the bread. Put on your sliced turkey and make a
sandwich.

Fried Chicken

*"Nobody taught me how to make fried chicken. I just
picked it up by experience. I just knowed you got to put
grease in the skillet to fry chicken. Some things you just
think, 'Well, I'm goin' to do it this way!'
And you just do it."*

chicken
salt
flour
pepper
paprika
Puritan oil

Put the chicken pieces in a big pot of water. Add two tablespoons of salt
for every one chicken that you use. Soak the chicken in the salty water
overnight in the refrigerator. The next day, drain off the water, pat the
chicken pieces dry.

Mix the flour (enough to coat all of the chicken) with the pepper and
the paprika and a little bit of salt to taste. Coat each piece of chicken with
this mixture.

In an iron skillet, add the Puritan oil and cook it until it sizzles. The
grease should be even up with the chicken. Then add a few pieces of
chicken and turn down the heat to medium. Cook the chicken a half hour
or so on one side and flip it and cook it a half hour on the other side until
it is evenly browned.

Remove the pieces from the pan as they are done and drain them on a
paper towel.

Chicken Broth

"People always come 'round my house asking for broth. 'You've got to give me some broth,' they say."

1 chicken
salt, plenty of it
red pepper
water

Put the chicken and the salt and red pepper in a pot. Add the water, but don't use very much. If you put a lot of water in you lose the taste of the chicken. Put in maybe a cup or two. Let the chicken simmer approximately 1-1/2 hours.

Chicken Casserole

*"This is good to have on hand in the freezer.
It will keep there indefinitely."*

1 chicken (6 pounds)
2 teaspoons salt
1/2 teaspoon pepper
1/2 cup chopped onion
2 stalks celery
2 medium green peppers, chopped
1 pound flat noodles
1/4 cup and 1 tablespoon flour
2 cups milk
2 (10-3/4 ounce) cans cream of mushroom soup
2 (2 ounce) jars chopped pimientos
1 clove mashed garlic
1 teaspoon garlic powder
1 teaspoon Worcestershire sauce
1/2 cup sherry
3 cups Velveeta cheese
3 (4 ounce) cans sliced mushrooms
3 cups Cheddar cheese, grated
3/4 cup Parmesan cheese
sliced almonds

Place the chicken in a pot, barely cover with water, and add the salt and pepper. Bring the water to a boil, then reduce the heat and put a cover on. Cook until tender, about one hour. When the chicken is cool, remove the meat. Save the broth for the casserole.

Chop up the onion, celery, and the green peppers. Put these in the large pot with the chicken broth and cook lightly for about 15 minutes until tender. Dump the noodles in the broth with the vegetables and add just enough water to cover. Cook for several minutes. Add the flour and stir until the broth is smooth. Cook for one minute. Gradually stir in the milk. Then add the soup, pimientos, mashed garlic, garlic powder,

Worcestershire sauce, sherry, chicken meat, the Velveeta cheese, and two of the three cans of mushrooms along with their juice. Mix well and cook over medium heat for ten minutes. Remove from the heat and let the mixture completely cool so all the flavors can mingle. Grease two large baking pans. Pour in the casserole. Top with the Cheddar and Parmesan cheeses, sliced almonds, and the remaining mushrooms, drained of their liquid. Bake at 350° for ten minutes until hot and bubbly.

This will make enough casserole to fill two dishes, each serving six to eight people.

Spicy Beef Roast with Gravy

"Everybody loves this. I got the recipe from
Mrs. Anna L. Pittman."

1 (2-4 pound) rib or rump roast
6 ounces chili sauce
5 ounces ketchup
2 or 3 slices lemon
1 green pepper, chopped
1 onion, chopped
1 can (15 ounces) mushrooms
1/2 cup water
1/2 teaspoon sugar

Preheat the oven to 325°. Mix all of the ingredients together and pour over the roast. Cover the roast with foil, and seal tightly. Cook about one hour and forty-five minutes to two hours, depending on the size of your roast. When the time is up, turn off the oven with the roast still in it and let it sit there for an hour or two until the oven cools.

Roast Beef

"I marinate this with everything in the kitchen!"

1 sirloin tip or bottom round (any size)
brown sugar
soy sauce
Worcestershire sauce
garlic salt
salt
red pepper

Put the roast in a bowl. Mix up the other ingredients separately, then spread on the meat on both sides. Cover and put in the refrigerator overnight, but remember to turn the meat over every few hours.

Before roasting, take the meat out and lay it on a big piece of Reynolds Wrap. Pour the juices on top and wrap the roast up tight. Stick a meat thermometer in the center and roast the meat in a preheated 350° oven according to your taste. I fix mine at medium. This takes several hours depending on the size of the roast. It runs about 20 to 25 minutes per pound.

Roast Beef on Buns or Bread

roast beef, sliced
bite-sized buns or slices of rye bread with the crust removed
1 (10 ounces) Durkee Famous Sandwich and Salad Sauce
1 teaspoon horseradish
2 teaspoons Dijon mustard

Mix your Durkee sauce with the horseradish and mustard. Spread on the buns or bread and lay the roast beef on top. If you're not serving the sandwiches that day, put them together without the sauce and serve the sauce as an accompaniment.

Meat Loaf

"This makes enough for fifty. I had this at church once when we had a conference. They liked it. It's got all that seasoning. They said, 'Oh, this is good meat loaf!'"

3 medium onions
1/2 cup green pepper
4 cups fresh bread crumbs
2 cups milk
3 eggs, beaten
2 tablespoons Worcestershire sauce
1/2 teaspoon pepper
1/2 teaspoon basil
1-1/2 teaspoons sage
1-1/2 teaspoons paprika
1/2 teaspoon nutmeg
4 tablespoons chopped parsley
1-1/2 teaspoons salt
1/2 teaspoon thyme
1-1/2 teaspoons poultry seasoning
3 pounds ground pork
3 pounds lean hamburger
6 slices bacon

Chop up the onions and the green pepper in a food processor. Put them in a big bowl with all the other ingredients and mix well. Divide the meat into three balls and put it in three greased loaf pans. Lay three slices of bacon on each meat loaf. Sprinkle some paprika on top. Bake at 350° for an hour and fifteen minutes. Each loaf serves eight people. Extra loaves can be frozen.

Breads

Thelma's Rolls

"I've been doing these about forty-five years. I try to keep them in the house all the time. I make seventeen or eighteen dozen every week, sometimes more, 'cause people just call and say, 'You got any rolls?' Or they ring the doorbell and say 'You got any rolls?' I charge a dollar a dozen. . . . When you stir the yeast up with the warm water it should bubble up. If it don't, somethin's not right. When you roll your dough out, don't go over it back and forth, that does somethin' to it. You got to roll from the center out in one direction all the way around until your dough is about a half inch thick."

4 packages Rapid-Rise yeast
pinch of sugar
2 cups warm water
4 eggs
2 sticks (1 cup) butter
1 cup Crisco
2 teaspoons salt
not quite 2 cups sugar
2 cups boiling water
16 cups White Lily all-purpose flour
melted butter

Put a pinch of sugar in a bowl. Heat the two cups of warm water until about 110°. Pour it in the bowl. Add the yeast and stir well, approximately one minute until the yeast is dissolved and bubbles up. In another bowl, put in the eggs and beat them with a mixer until stiff, approximately five minutes. In another bowl, beat the butter, Crisco, salt, and sugar on medium until the mixture gets really creamy, about three to five minutes. Turn the mixer to low speed and add the boiling water. When that is all mixed in, turn the mixer back up slightly and add the stiff eggs. When that is well mixed, add the yeast, turn up the mixer a little more and mix for thirty seconds to one minute.

Spread out a piece of wax paper or aluminum foil and sift the flour out onto it. Measure out four cups, add to the yeast mixture and mix by hand vigorously for two minutes until the flour is well blended. Add the rest of the flour four cups at a time, beating vigorously by hand for two minutes or so after each addition. When all the flour is in, beat the dough well by hand, scraping it up from the bottom of the bowl with a spatula with one hand, while rotating the bowl with the other hand. Brush the top of the dough with softened or melted butter or margarine. Cover the bowl well with foil and let sit several hours until the dough has doubled in size. Put in the refrigerator overnight.

The next day, melt three to four sticks of margarine or butter in a saucepan and set aside. Take out about a fifth of the dough and knead it with as little flour as possible. Don't bear down on the bread. Knead it gently and quickly. Roll it out a half inch thick and cut with a biscuit cutter. Grease the bottom of a pan with melted butter Dip each roll in the melted butter and place in the pan so it lightly touches the other rolls. Roll out the rest of the dough. Let the rolls sit in the pans about three hours while they rise.

Bake at 375° for 15 minutes.

Makes 16 to 17 dozen, depending on the activity of the yeast and the eggs, the thickness of the dough, and the size of the biscuit cutter.

Biscuits

"You can use any size cutter you want. I did make some for a girl for her wedding with a heart-shape cutter."

2 cups flour
2 heaping teaspoons baking powder
1/2 teaspoon baking soda
1 tablespoon sugar
l teaspoon salt
1/4 cup Crisco
3/4 cup buttermilk

Preheat the oven to 450°. Mix up the ingredients. Roll out the dough on a floured board. Work in more flour if the dough is too moist. Cut out with a cutter. Place on a greased tray or pan and set in oven with rack adjusted to the second rung from the top. Cook about eight minutes until golden brown.

Makes roughly 30 biscuits.

Salt Rising Bread

*"This recipe is real old, about 100 years, at least. It's a bread that is not
a lot of trouble, but you do have to be at home with it. I ferment the
potatoes in a half gallon jar which I wrap with linen sacks and put in a
kettle of warm water. When it is ready, a foam comes to the top. If there
is no foam, it's no good. When you smell it in the beginning, you would
not want to eat it. But when you mix it up with the other
ingredients and it's cooked, it's real good."*

2 medium potatoes, peeled and grated
2 heaping tablespoons cornmeal
2 heaping tablespoons sugar
2 teaspoons salt
3 cups boiling water
1 cup milk
1 heaping tablespoon Crisco
2 teaspoons baking powder
1 teaspoon baking soda
flour, enough to make a stiff batter but not too stiff

Put the potatoes, the meal, the sugar, the salt and the boiling water in a
half gallon jar and keep warm overnight. The next day, strain the foam off
the mixture, keep the liquid, and discard the rest.

Let the milk come just to a simmer before adding the Crisco, the baking
powder and the baking soda. Add the fermented liquid and mix. Put the
mixture in a big bowl. Add enough flour to make a stiff batter which you
can beat. Let rise in a warm place to double the size. Then add more flour
to make the dough a little stiffer. Shape into three loaves and let rise to
double in size. Bake at 350° for one hour.

Vegetables

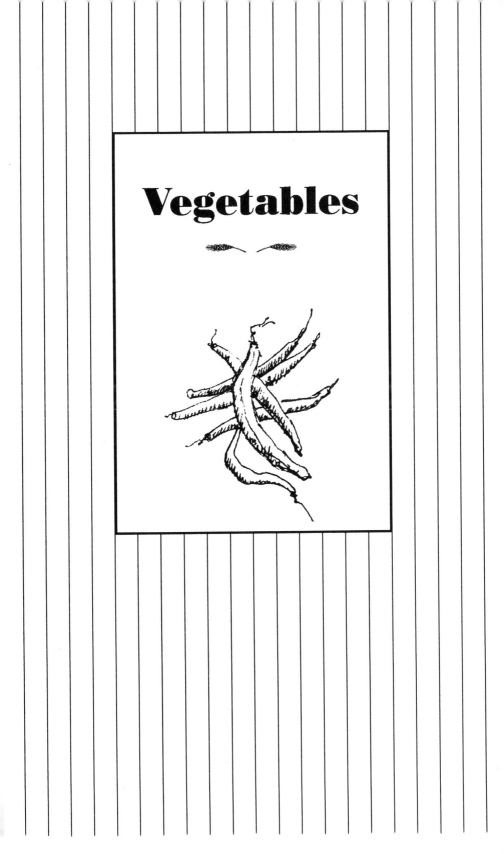

Potatoes Au Gratin

"I use a good cooking potato for this. I really like Ida-hoes. But you have to be careful and don't let them cook up too much. They cook up real quick. 'Course you can use any kind of white potato."

16 potatoes
salt
1 small onion
red pepper

Cheese Sauce:
1 stick (8 tablespoons) butter
4 tablespoons flour
2 cups milk
1/2 pound Velveeta cheese
sharp Cheddar cheese, grated

Use two potatoes per person. Peel and dice the potatoes. Put them in a pot and barely cover them with water. Add a pinch of salt. Let the potatoes cook until just tender. Drain them if there is water still in the pot. Put the potatoes in a casserole. Chop up about a tablespoon of onions and add to the potatoes. Put in a pinch of cayenne pepper.

Make the cheese sauce by melting the butter in a saucepan, then stir in the flour and cook, stirring for two minutes. Pour in the milk. Cook, stirring, until thick.

When the sauce is thick, add the Velveeta. Stir until the cheese melts. Pour the sauce over the potatoes. Cover the casserole with grated sharp Cheddar cheese. Bake at 350° until the casserole bubbles, approximately 15 minutes.

Serves eight.

Mashed Potatoes

"The secret of mashed potatoes is heating the milk and the butter. I use White Russet potatoes. Red ones don't do too well. They stay too firm. Peel your potatoes (about two per person) and cook in salted water. Beat your potatoes in the mixer. The more you beat them, the better they are."

potatoes
salt, to taste
milk, to taste
butter, to taste

Easter

Country Ham

Potatoes Au Gratin

Broccoli Casserole

Corn Pudding

Tomato Aspic

Rolls

Fruit Bowl

Angel Food Cake

Sweet Potatoes with Bourbon

"These are good! I use Maker's Mark bourbon.
This is Mrs. Ruth Ingram's recipe."

3 cups sweet potatoes, cooked, peeled, and mashed
1 cup sugar
1 stick (8 tablespoons) butter, melted
2 eggs, beaten
1 teaspoon vanilla
1/3 cup milk
1 teaspoon bourbon

Topping:
    1/2 cup brown sugar
    1/4 cup flour
    1/2 stick butter
    1/2 cup pecans, chopped

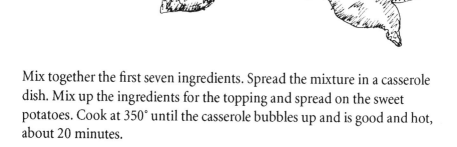

Mix together the first seven ingredients. Spread the mixture in a casserole dish. Mix up the ingredients for the topping and spread on the sweet potatoes. Cook at 350° until the casserole bubbles up and is good and hot, about 20 minutes.

Serves eight.

Corn Pudding

"I use frozen white Shupeg corn, although you can use fresh corn, too, about two cups."

4 eggs
4 tablespoons sugar
4 tablespoons flour
1 teaspoon salt
2 cups milk
1/2 stick (4 tablespoons) butter
2 cups corn

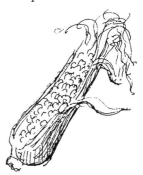

Preheat the oven to 350°. Beat together the eggs first until they are stiff. In a separate bowl mix all the other ingredients (the butter can be sliced into pieces) and then add the eggs. Put in a casserole dish and bake for 45 minutes. While baking, stir twice, once after the first 15 minutes, then again 15 minutes later.

Serves six.

Christmas Dinner

Cheese Straws
Roast Turkey with Gravy and Dressing
Country Ham
Cranberry Salad with Celery Sticks
Peas
Corn Pudding
Rolls
Kentucky Pecan Cake

Green Beans

"Half Runners are my favorite bean, but Kentucky Wonders will do, too. I use a pepper pod from the garden to season....There's a girl in town who brings her cooked beans by so I can season 'em, but she says they still don't taste like mine. Then I found out what she done. She was stirring 'em and addin' more water. You're not supposed to stir green beans. When I put mine on, I let them cook about three hours. Well, after they've cooked about two hours, you might take a fork or spoon and just kinda turn 'em over from the bottom lightly. And you're supposed to start with enough water that you don't have to add water and cook 'em real slow. Stirring 'em I think does something to them."

beans, however many you want
sugar, to taste
salt, to taste
pepper
tiny piece of chili pepper pod
seasoning bacon or salt pork
onion, to taste

Snip the ends off the beans. Cut them in half. Remove the strings. Slice up the onion. Add all of the ingredients in a big kettle, and season the beans to your taste. Cover the beans with water. Put a top on the kettle and simmer slowly for three or four hours. For the last half hour turn up the heat and let the water cook out of the beans. Adjust the seasoning if need be.

Broccoli Casserole

"Most of the time I use chopped frozen broccoli which I let steam for a few minutes. But fresh broccoli is fine, too."

steamed broccoli—1 (16 ounce) package or two heads
of fresh broccoli
1 stick (8 tablespoons) butter
4 tablespoons flour
2 cups milk
1/2 pound Velveeta cheese
sharp Cheddar cheese, grated

Make the cheese sauce by melting the butter in a saucepan, then stir in the flour and cook, stirring for two minutes. Pour in the milk. Cook, stirring, until thick. When the sauce is thick add the Velveeta. Stir until the cheese melts. Pour the sauce over the steamed broccoli. Cover the casserole with grated sharp Cheddar cheese. Bake at 350° until the casserole bubbles, approximately 15 minutes.

Serves eight.

Mixed Vegetable Casserole

"People just rave about this recipe when I bring it to church."

1 large package frozen mixed vegetables
1 can asparagus tips, chopped
1 roll garlic cheese
1 can cream of mushroom soup
snack crackers or bread crumbs

Preheat the oven to 350°. Cook frozen vegetables in salted water. Drain. Add the asparagus tips and mix well. Combine the cheese and the mushroom soup in a pan and warm over low heat. In a casserole dish alternate the layers of vegetables with the soup-cheese sauce. Top the casserole with crushed crackers. Bake until the casserole is bubbly and golden brown, approximately 30 minutes.

Serves eight.

Family Dinner

Cheese Straws
Meat Loaf
Mixed Vegetable Casserole
Frozen Fruit Salad
Rolls
Lynda B. Johnson Chocolate Cake

Salads

Thelma's Tomato Aspic

"When people ask me to make this for a party, I ask them 'Are you goin' to have men there?' 'cause aspic is not a favorite with men. I don't know why they don't like it, but I know they don't eat it. Now women do like it. It used to be a favorite of mine, but I got tired of it. It used to be I couldn't get enough. I got so now I don't care to think about it. I guess I eat too much of it."

1 package Knox gelatin
1 (46 ounce) can tomato juice
1 heaping teaspoon horseradish
1 scant teaspoon Dijon mustard
2 (3 ounce) packages lemon Jello
juice of one lemon
salt to taste (I put a pinch.)
1 teaspoon tarragon vinegar
2 teaspoons dill weed
green olives, sliced
green onions, chopped
celery, chopped
green pepper, chopped

Put the gelatin in a small bowl and pour a little of the tomato juice over that. In another bowl put in the horseradish and mustard and pour a little tomato juice over that. In a large saucepan put in remaining tomato juice and bring to a boil. Take the pan off the stove, add the lemon Jello and stir until it dissolves. To this add the lemon juice, the salt, and the tomato juice mixtures in the two small bowls. Pour this mixture into a mold. Let it cool slightly. Put in the vegetables. Chill. Unmold by wetting a dish rag in warm water and wiping over the bottom. Serve with mayonnaise.

Fourth of July Bean Salad

"I only make this salad for the Fourth of July Shakertown boat ride. It serves 12. I make it the day before and let it sit overnight."

1 (16 ounce) can kidney beans
1 (16 ounce) can green beans
1 (16 ounce) can lima beans
1 (16 ounce) can wax beans
1 (16 ounce) can butter beans
onions, to taste
1 medium green pepper, thinly sliced

Dressing:

3/4 cup sugar	1/2 teaspoon salt
1/2 cup vinegar	1/2 teaspoon pepper
1/2 cup salad oil	1 tablespoon minced parsley

Combine the beans, onion, and green pepper. Toss. Mix the dressing and heat. Let it come to a boil and stir until the sugar dissolves. Pour while hot over the beans. Chill several hours or overnight.

Fourth of July Shakertown Boat Ride Picnic Boxes

Fried Chicken

Potato Salad

Fourth of July Bean Salad

Rolls

Lemon Bars

Fresh Fruit

Potato Salad

"For my potato salad I like to use White Russets best. You can use most any kind, but don't use white Idahoes. I cook the potatoes first and peel them while they are warm. Don't overcook them!"

5 pounds potatoes	lemon pepper
1 small green pepper	mayonnaise
1/2 stalk celery	Marzetti Slaw Dressing
sweet pickle	Cooked Dressing
6 hard-boiled eggs	1 small jar pimientos
salt	

Cook and peel the potatoes. Chop the green pepper, celery, and sweet pickle. Slice the eggs. Mix the ingredients well while the potatoes are warm, adding the mayonnaise, the Marzetti Slaw Dressing, and the Cooked Dressing in proportions according to your taste. Add seasonings to taste. Put in the refrigerator and let sit overnight.

Cooked Dressing

"This is good for salads. I used to always make my own mayonnaise for everything too, but I don't do that anymore on account of the salmonella in the egg yolk. But this is real good with store-bought mayonnaise. It keeps a long time in the refrigerator. I always have some there."

1 pint vinegar
2 dozen egg yolks
3 cups sugar

Combine the ingredients in a double boiler and cook until thick. Let cool. Store in a jar in the refrigerator. It will keep there for two to three weeks. When you get ready to use it, mix it, half and half with mayonnaise.

Layer Salad

*"This is a meal within itself. I do it at church a lot. They
have a fit over it down there. Everybody grabs it. Make
this the night before."*

1 head of iceberg lettuce
1/2 bunch of celery, chopped
1 medium onion, chopped or sliced
1 green pepper, chopped or sliced
2 or 3 carrots, grated
1 (10 ounce) package frozen peas
4 hard boiled eggs, chopped or sliced
1 cup mayonnaise or more, to taste
1 tablespoon sugar
1/2 cup grated Cheddar cheese
8-10 pieces crumbled bacon

Remove the outer leaves of the lettuce and discard. Wash the remaining
head and cut it up into shreds. Put a third of the lettuce into a large bowl.
Sprinkle half of the celery, onion, carrots, pepper, peas, and eggs on top.
Add another layer of lettuce. Put the rest of the chopped ingredients on
top of this. Cover with the remaining lettuce. Mix the mayonnaise and the
sugar together and spread on top. Sprinkle the cheddar cheese over the
mayonnaise followed by the crumbled bacon. Let sit overnight in the
refrigerator.

Chicken Salad

*"This makes a little better than a quart which is enough
to serve eight people. Take the chicken off the bone while
it is warm if you can, because it is a little easier to do."*

1 frying chicken (approximately 4 pounds)
salt
red pepper
1/2 bunch celery
1 small jar pimientos
1/2 cup slivered almonds
2 ounces tidbit pineapple
1 tablespoon sweet relish
mayonnaise
Marzetti Slaw Dressing
Cooked Dressing (see recipe page 68)

Put the chicken, salt, and pepper with some water in a pot. Boil gently
until the chicken is tender, but not so much that it falls off the bone
(about one hour). Take the meat off the bone and refrigerate it until it
gets good and cold.

Chop up the celery and add it along with the remaining ingredients to
the cold chicken. Add enough mayonnaise to make the salad moist. Put in
a little bit of Marzetti Slaw Dressing and a little bit of cooked dressing.
Mix well. Add more salt and pepper if necessary.

Frozen Fruit Salad

"Let this salad sit for several hours in the refrigerator so the flavors can mingle before freezing. In the winter time when fresh fruit is not available this salad can be made with fruit cocktail, pineapple chunks, and red and green cherries."

1/2 pint heavy cream
1 cup mayonnaise
1 (8 ounce) package cream cheese
fresh fruit in season: cantaloupe, honeydew, grapes, peaches, strawberries, etc.
a handful of marshmallows

Beat together the heavy cream, mayonnaise, and cream cheese. Cut up the fruit and add it along with the marshmallows to the cream mixture. Put in the refrigerator for several hours then freeze.

Red Salad

"*People call for this at their parties all the time. 'Thelma,' they say, 'we want that red salad!' I don't know why, really. I guess it does go well with a lot of things.*"

cantaloupe, strawberries, grapes, peaches, canned pineapple
lemon Jello (6 ounces)
mixed fruit Jello (6 ounces)

Wash and cut up the fruit. Make the Jello. After it begins to set, add the fruit. Refrigerate.

Cranberry Salad

"*I keep chicken casserole and cranberry salad frozen all the time. They are good to have on hand in case somebody dies. The cranberry salad you can eat with any meat.*"

6 ounces cream cheese
2 tablespoons mayonnaise
2 tablespoons sugar
1 pound cranberry sauce
1 (9 ounce) can crushed pineapple
1/2 cup pecans
2 cups Cool Whip

Mix together all of the ingredients and let sit overnight. Put the salad into containers and freeze it indefinitely.

Cakes,
Pies, and
Cookies

Angel Food Cake

"I don't know if anybody makes their angel food cake like this. I sift the flour nine times. That's an old-fashioned way. I started doing it like this and I keep on doing it. You can do it on a mixer, but I don't like it, so I don't do it. To me the cake comes out heavy. As soon as the cake comes out of the oven, I turn it upside down and I think 'Please, don't fall out!' If it falls out, it isn't right, but I haven't had one fall out in a long time."

1-1/2 cups egg whites (about a dozen large eggs depending on the size of the eggs. I use large eggs and I measure.)
pinch of salt
1-1/4 teaspoon cream of tartar
1-3/4 cups sugar
1-1/4 cups Swan's Down enriched cake flour sifted nine times mixed with 1/2 cup of the sugar
1/2 teaspoon almond extract
1 teaspoon vanilla

Beat the egg whites with the pinch of salt until they begin to foam. Add the cream of tartar. Beat until stiff—that is till they hold a peak. Beat in one and a quarter cups sugar adding four tablespoons at a time, counting 24 beats each time you add. Then fold in the flour and sugar mixture, four tablespoons at a time, counting fourteen strokes each time you add. For the last four tablespoons, count twenty-four strokes.

Put the batter in a tube pan. Don't grease the pan or anything, just sprinkle a little flour in beforehand.

Bake at 350° for 35-40 minutes. When the cake is cool, work a knife around the edge to loosen. Frost with Seven Minute Frosting.

Seven Minute Frosting

2 egg whites
1-1/2 cups sugar
1/3 cup water
1 teaspoon Karo Syrup
1 tablespoon powdered sugar
1 teaspoon vanilla

Combine the first four ingredients and cook in a double boiler for seven minutes. Beat while cooking. Remove from the stove, add the powdered sugar and vanilla and beat until it is thick enough to spread.

Stuffed Angel Food Cake

"This is the same thing as the angel food cake, only when it is cold, cut the top off, and hull the cake out. Don't throw the cake insides out, though. I crumb it up and put it in my filling. Whip a pint of whipping cream. Add cherries, marshmallows, about two handfuls. If you have strawberries, you can put them in. I add one small can of pineapple tidbits, too. I mix all of this up, then I stuff the angel food cake and put the top back on. I ice it with Seven Minute Frosting and keep it in the refrigerator."

Chocolate Angel Food Cake

"I made this at the Walker's a lot. It's coarser than the white cake."

1-1/2 cups egg whites (approximately 1 dozen eggs)
1/4 teaspoon salt
1 teaspoon cream of tartar
2 cups sugar
1/2 teaspoon lemon juice
1 teaspoon vanilla
1 cup flour
1/2 cup cocoa
1 teaspoon baking powder

Beat the egg whites with the salt until creamy. Then add the cream of tartar and beat until stiff. Fold in the sugar, lemon juice and vanilla. Sift the flour, cocoa, and baking powder three times. Fold into the egg white mixture. Pour into an ungreased stem pan and bake at 350° for one hour.

American Red Velvet Cake

"My beautician, Myrtle, gave me this. I don't know what it come out of. When I used to go to her beauty parlor, she knew I liked to cook, so she'd always give me cookbooks while I was under the dryer. She'd give me paper, and I would sit there and copy recipes....It's a good choice for a Valentine's Day dessert. Make the frosting before starting the cake."

Frosting:

8 tablespoons flour	2 sticks (1 cup) butter
2 cups milk	vanilla, a teaspoon or so, to taste
1 cup Crisco	2 cups sugar

Mix together the flour and the milk in a saucepan and cook over medium heat until thick. Let stand until cool. Cream the Crisco and the butter with the vanilla and sugar. Beat until fluffy then add the cooled flour mixture. Beat well. Cut the cooled, cooked cake in four layers, then frost heavily between the layers and all over the sides.

Cake:

2 ounces red food coloring	1 tablespoon vanilla
3 tablespoons instant milk cocoa	2-1/2 cups flour
1/2 cup Crisco	1 cup buttermilk
1-1/2 cups sugar	1 teaspoon baking soda
2 eggs	1 tablespoon vinegar
1/2 teaspoon salt	

Preheat the oven to 350°. Using a mixer, mix the food coloring with the cocoa and let stand. In a separate bowl mix the Crisco with the sugar until creamy. Add the eggs and the coloring mixture. Mix well. Add the salt and the vanilla, mixing well. Add the flour and the buttermilk alternately. By hand add the baking soda and then vinegar and stir. Pour into two greased and floured cake pans. Bake for 35 to 40 minutes.

Lynda B. Johnson Chocolate Cake

"I got this out of the newspaper back when Mr. Johnson was President. People love this cake."

4 ounces semi-sweet chocolate
1/2 cup boiling water
2-1/2 cups sifted flour
4 egg whites
2 sticks (1 cup) butter
2 cups sugar
1/4 teaspoon salt
4 egg yolks
1 teaspoon baking soda
1 cup buttermilk

Preheat the oven to 350°. Grease and flour two round cake pans or one large sheet pan. Dissolve the chocolate in the boiling water. In a big bowl sift the flour three times. In a separate bowl beat the egg whites until stiff. In still another bowl, cream the butter, sugar and salt. Add the egg yolks one at a time to the creamed butter mixture. Then add the dissolved chocolate. In still one more bowl dissolve the baking soda in the buttermilk. Then add the sifted flour alternating with the buttermilk and soda beginning and ending with the flour to the chocolate batter. Finally, fold in the egg whites. Pour into the round cake pans or the sheet pan and bake for 45 minutes.

You can use either mocha or caramel icing when the cake is completely cool.

Mocha Icing

3/4 stick (6 tablespoons) butter
2-1/2 cups powdered sugar
strong coffee
2 tablespoons cocoa

Beat the ingredients together using enough coffee to thin down the mixture. Ice the cake.

Caramel Icing

1-1/2 cups brown sugar
1 stick (8 tablespoons) butter
1/3 cup cream
1-1/2 cups confectioner's sugar

Mix the first three ingredients in a saucepan. Put on the stove. Cook at medium heat until it thickens and browns, about four minutes. Let cool. Beat into the mixture 1-1/2 cups confectioner's sugar until thick enough to spread. If too thick, add more cream.

White Butter Cake

"I got this recipe from Margaret Mundy. It was her grand-mother's wedding cake. It makes a big, light, fluffy cake...I make dressing out of the egg yolks or I turn around and make a yellow cake by the same recipe. 'Course you beat your egg yolks just like you do your egg whites. And you have to use the creamy butter, 'cause I give it to somebody and they said, 'you know it don't work with margarine.' And I said 'No. You're supposed to use creamy butter. That means <u>butter</u>. That don't mean margarine....'"

8 egg whites
2 sticks (1 cup) butter
2 cups white sugar
1 teaspoon vanilla
4 cups flour
4 teaspoons baking powder
pinch salt
1 cup milk

Preheat the oven to 350°. Grease and flour two round cake pans or one pan for a large sheet cake. Beat the egg whites until stiff. In a separate bowl, cream the butter and the sugar until fluffy. Add the vanilla. Sift the flour, baking powder, and salt three times. Add the flour alternatively with the milk to the butter and sugar beginning and ending with the flour. Fold in the beaten egg whites. Bake for 45 minutes.
  Ice with your favorite icing.

Whipped Cream Pound Cake

"Very rich, but, oh, so good!"

1 cup whipping cream
2 sticks (1 cup) butter
3 cups sugar
2 teaspoons vanilla
3 cups flour
6 eggs, beaten

Oil and flour a large tube pan. Preheat the oven to 325°. Whip the cream until light and fluffy and set aside. Cream the butter with the sugar. Add the vanilla. Then add the flour and beaten eggs alternately. Beat well after each addition. Fold in the whipping cream. Bake for 1 1/4 hours. Remove the cake from the pan when cool.

Basic Two Egg Cake

"I made this one day when I was cake-hungry, and it was so good, I ate the whole cake...over several days that is. This cake can be dressed up in a lot of different ways. Top it with fresh, sweetened strawberries, or peaches and whipped cream. Top it with bananas and powdered sugar. You can even make blueberry muffins with it. Pour the batter into muffin tins until 3/4 full. Add blueberries to each muffin. Bake at 375° for 15-20 minutes."

1 stick (1/2 cup) butter
1 cup sugar
2 eggs
1/4 teaspoon salt
2-1/4 teaspoons baking powder
2-1/4 cup flour, sifted
3/4 cup milk

Cream the butter and sugar. Add the eggs, one at a time, mixing well. In a separate bowl, combine the dry ingredients. Add them alternating with the milk to the butter-sugar-egg mixture. Pour into two greased and floured square pans. Bake at 375° for 20-25 minutes until done.

Women's Club Luncheon

Chicken Salad
Mixed Vegetable Casserole
Red Salad
Gingerbread with Lemon Sauce

Pineapple Upside Down Cake

1 stick (8 tablespoons) butter
1 cup brown sugar
1 large can of pineapple, crushed or in pieces.
1 Basic Two Egg Cake (see recipe on preceding page)

Melt the butter. Pour in an oblong cake pan. Sprinkle the sugar on top, then spread out the pineapple. Pour in the batter for the Basic Two Egg Cake. Bake at 375° for 45 minutes. Flip the cake over onto a serving dish as soon as you take it out of the oven.

Gingerbread with Lemon Sauce

"I take the notion for gingerbread for myself 'bout once a year, usually in the winter. That's really the only time I make it. You don't have people calling for it too much anymore. It's an old-fashioned dessert."

1/2 cup margarine
1/4 cup packed brown sugar
1 egg
1/2 cup sorghum molasses
1-1/2 cups White Lily all-purpose flour
3/4 teaspoon ground ginger
3/4 teaspoon ground cinnamon
1/2 teaspoon baking powder
1/2 teaspoon baking soda
1/2 teaspoon salt
1/2 cup boiling water

Preheat the oven to 350°. Grease and flour lightly a round or a square pan. Beat the margarine and the brown sugar together until it's real creamy and light. Add the egg and the molasses and beat well. Stir together the flour, spices, baking powder, baking soda and the salt. Then add this alternately with the boiling water to the creamed mixture, beating all the while. Pour into the pan and bake for 30-35 minutes. Serve with lemon sauce.

Lemon Sauce:

1/2 cup sugar	1 cup water
1 tablespoon cornstarch	2 tablespoons butter
1/8 teaspoon salt	2 tablespoons lemon juice
1/8 teaspoon nutmeg	

Mix the first five ingredients. Cook and stir until thick and bubbly. Stir in the butter and lemon juice.

Prune Cake with Buttermilk Icing

"We used to have this a lot with whipped cream on top for dinner at church."

2 cups flour	3 eggs
1 teaspoon soda	1 cup Wesson oil
1 teaspoon cinnamon	1-1/2 cups sugar
1 teaspoon allspice	1 cup buttermilk
1 teaspoon nutmeg	1 cup cooked, pitted prunes, cut up
1 teaspoon salt	1 cup chopped pecans

Preheat the oven to 350°. Grease a tube pan with Crisco and flour it.Sift all of the dry ingredients. Add everything else but the prunes and the pecans and mix with a mixer. When it is well mixed, stir in the prunes and the pecans. Cook for 40 to 50 minutes until done. Let cool. Frost.

Icing:

1 cup sugar	1 tablespoon dark corn syrup
1/2 cup buttermilk	1/4 cup margarine
1 teaspoon soda	

Mix everything up good. Put in a saucepan and bring to a rolling boil. Remove from the stove and beat the sauce slightly. Pour over cooled cake.

Applesauce Cake

"This cake is good! It can be used for muffins, too, which are nice to serve for brunch along with Sausage Casserole. Allow 30 minutes for the muffins to cook. That's the only difference. I make my muffins with paper liners."

2 sticks (1 cup) butter
2 cups white sugar
1 egg, well-beaten
2 cups applesauce
1 teaspoon cinnamon
1/2 teaspoon nutmeg
1-3/4 teaspoon baking soda
1 teaspoon vanilla
1 cup nuts
1 cup raisins
3 cups flour

Preheat the oven to 300°. Cream the butter. Add the sugar. Beat the egg until frothy and add to the butter-sugar mixture. Then add the applesauce, and the dry ingredients. Add the vanilla. Fold in the nuts, raisins, and flour. Bake for one hour in an oblong pan or in layer pans which have been greased and floured.

Christmas Day Breakfast

Sausage Casserole
Sliced Country Ham
Toasted Salt Rising Bread
Applesauce Cake Muffins
Zucchini Bread with Pineapple

Zucchini Cake

"This is a real cake, not a bread. It's real moist and good."

Cake:
   3 cups flour
   3 cups sugar
   1 teaspoon salt
   1-1/2 teaspoons baking soda
   4 tablespoons cocoa
   1 teaspoon vanilla
   4 eggs
   1-1/2 cups Puritan oil
   1 cup chopped nuts
   3 cups grated zucchini

Frosting:
   1 (8 ounce) package cream cheese
   1 stick Oleo
   1 pound powdered sugar
   1/2 teaspoon vanilla

Preheat the oven to 325°. Grease and flour a 13"x 9" pan or three 9" pans or four 8"x 8" pans. In a big bowl mix together real well all of the cake ingredients adding the grated zucchini last. Pour into the prepared cake pan or pans and bake about 35 minutes depending on the size of the pan. Remove from the oven and let cool.

   Mix all of the frosting ingredients together and beat until fluffy. Spread onto the cooled cake.

Zucchini Bread With Pineapple

"This is Mrs. Hachett's recipe. It's good and moist. You can use this for muffins, too. Cook them about 30 minutes."

3 eggs, beaten
2 cups sugar
1 cup oil
2 teaspoons vanilla
3 cups flour
2 teaspoons soda
1 teaspoon salt
1/2 teaspoon baking powder
1-1/2 teaspoons cinnamon
2 cups grated zucchini
3/4 cup chopped walnuts
1 (8 ounce) can crushed pineapple, well drained

Preheat the oven to 350°. Beat up the eggs until frothy, add the sugar, then the oil and the vanilla. Sift the dry ingredients together then fold them into the sugar mixture. Fold in the zucchini, nuts and pineapple. Bake for one hour in two 9"x5"x3" pans which have been greased and floured.

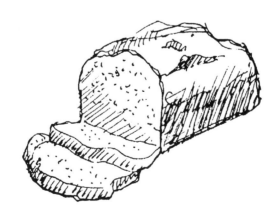

Pecan Cake

"I make this at Christmas. I use sorghum and Maker's Mark bourbon."

1 stick (8 tablespoons) butter
2 cups sugar
6 eggs, separated
4 cups flour, sifted
1 teaspoon baking powder
2 teaspoons nutmeg
1 cup bourbon
1/2 teaspoon baking soda
1-1/2 tablespoons sorghum or dark molasses
2 pounds white raisins
1 (16 ounce) box dates
1-1/2 pounds pecans
1/2 pound candied cherries, sliced
2 rings pineapple, diced

Grease and flour a tube pan. Preheat the oven to 275°.

Cream the butter and gradually add the sugar and the six egg yolks. Sift the flour, the baking powder and the nutmeg. Add it gradually to the butter mixture. Then add the bourbon, the soda, and the sorghum and mix well. Beat the egg whites until stiff and fold them into the batter. Dust the remaining ingredients lightly with flour and mix them gently into the batter. Pour the batter into the greased and floured pan and place in the oven on the middle rack. On the bottom rack beneath it, set a pan of water for steam. Cook for 3-1/2 hours.

Let the cake get cold before unmolding it. Then pour on enough bourbon until the cake is good and moist. Wrap up tightly in cheese cloth and then in Reynolds Wrap. It will keep a long time like this.

Kentucky Pecan Cake

"This is a real, real old recipe, perhaps 100 years old. Mrs. Ingram loves this cake. She has me put in two pounds of pecans and one pound of raisins. I use Maker's Mark bourbon in it."

6 eggs, beaten
1 pound sugar
2 sticks (1 cup) butter
4 cups flour
2 grated nutmegs (2 teaspoons to 2 tablespoons according to your taste)
2 pounds raisins
1 pound pecans
1 pound pitted dates
1 cup bourbon
1 teaspoon baking powder
1/2 teaspoon baking soda dissolved in 1/4 cup warm water

Preheat the oven to 350°. Grease and flour a large cake pan or several smaller loaf pans. Mix all of the ingredients up together real well. Pour the batter into the greased and floured pan and place in the oven on the middle rack. On the bottom rack beneath it, set a pan of water for steam. Cook for 3-1/2 hours.

Let the cake get cold before unmolding it. Then pour on enough bourbon until the cake is good and moist. Wrap up tightly in cheese cloth and then in Reynolds Wrap. It will keep a long time like this.

Five Pie Crusts

"I always make five pie crusts at a time. You can freeze the dough, but I never do. It gets used up too fast!"

5 cups flour
2 cups Crisco
1 teaspoon salt
1 egg
water
1 tablespoon white vinegar

Mix the flour, Crisco, and salt together until crumbly. In a measuring cup, beat the egg, then fill the cup up with water on top of the egg until the cup is 3/4 full. Add the vinegar. Beat up good. Gradually add this mixture to the flour mixture to form a smooth dough. Chill before rolling out.

Angel Pie

*"This is a pretty dessert. If you put sliced strawberries on top,
although it don't call for it, it makes it look especially pretty. It's not
hard to make. You can make it easy. Be sure to grease the pan
within anything else but butter or your crust will stick.
Use a deep dish pie pan."*

Crust:
   4 egg whites
   1/4 teaspoon cream of tartar
   1 cup sugar

Beat the egg whites until frothy. Add the cream of tartar and beat until
stiff. Add the sugar gradually and beat until glossy. Grease a deep dish pie
pan with any shortening other than butter. Sprinkle it with powdered
sugar. Pour the egg white mixture into the pie pan and bake at about 275°
for an hour. Let cool completely before adding the custard.

Custard:
   6 egg yolks
   grated rind of lemon
   5 tablespoons lemon juice
   5 tablespoons water
   3/4 cup sugar
   1-1/4 pints heavy cream

Beat the egg yolks until light and frothy. Add the lemon rind and juice
gradually, then slowly add the water and sugar. Cook in a double boiler
over boiling water until thick. This takes a little while, maybe 10 minutes
or so. When the custard is thick, take it off the stove and chill. When both
the custard and the crust are completely cool, whip the cream. Spread half
of the cream on the baked crust. Then cover with the custard and top
with the remaining cream. Refrigerate for several hours.

Chocolate Pie

"I don't know why, but this is one pie that always weeps over the top. If that happens, set the pie on a paper towel. And don't let that excite you. When the pie sits there and cools, it will be all right."

1 9" pie crust (see Five Pie Crusts recipe on page 90)

Filling:
   1-1/4 cups sugar
   1/2 cup corn starch
   3 ounces unsweetened chocolate
   3 cups milk
   4 eggs yolks
   vanilla
   3 tablespoons butter

Meringue Topping:
   4 egg whites
   8 tablespoons sugar

Preheat the oven to 400°. Poke a few holes in the pie crust. Bake the crust until golden brown.

Put the sugar, the corn starch, the three blocks of chocolate and the milk in a saucepan. Cook on medium heat until thick.

Separate the eggs, putting the whites aside for the meringue. Beat the four egg yolks. When the filling gets thick, take it off the heat and add several spoonfuls to the yolks, mixing well. Then add the yolks to the mixture in the saucepan. Put the saucepan back on the stove and cook, stirring, until the mixture gets good and thick. Put in a few drops of vanilla, and add three tablespoons of butter. Let that melt. Beat up the mixture, and then let it sit and cool.

In a separate bowl, gradually add a few tablespoons (two tablespoons per egg) of sugar to the egg whites while you beat them up until the whites are stiff.

Put the cooled chocolate mixture in the pie crust. Top with the meringue mixture. Bake at 350° for 15 minutes or until the top is golden brown.

Coconut Pie

1 9" pie crust (see Five Pie Crusts recipe on page 90)

Filling:
 1 cup sugar
 1/2 cup corn starch
 3 cups milk
 4 eggs yolks
 1-1/2 cups coconut
 1 teaspoon vanilla
 3 tablespoons butter

Meringue Topping:
 4 egg whites
 8 tablespoons sugar

Preheat the oven to 400°. Poke a few holes in the pie crust. Bake the crust until golden brown.

Put the sugar, the corn starch and the milk in a saucepan. Cook, stirring, until thick. Separate the four eggs, setting the whites aside for the meringue. Beat up the yolks. When the milk mixture is thick, remove from the stove. Add a few spoonfuls of it to the beaten egg yolks. Mix. Then put the egg yolks into the saucepan and return it to the heat. Cook the mixture some more until real thick (about two minutes). Remove from the stove.

Add the coconut, the vanilla, and the butter to the saucepan. Mix in until the butter melts. Cool the filling before pouring into the cooked pie crust.

To make the meringue topping, add the eight tablespoons of sugar gradually to the egg whites while you beat them. When they are stiff, pour them on top of the coconut mixture in the pie crust and put in the oven at 350° for 15 minutes or until the meringue is golden brown.

Butterscotch Pie

"I've been making this a long, long time. There's a man who says to me when he eats this it's like he's died and gone to heaven and then come back!"

1 9" pie crust (see Five Pie Crusts recipe on page 90)

Filling:
    1 cup brown sugar
    1 stick (8 tablespoons) butter
    4 tablespoons Half and Half cream
    6 level tablespoons flour
    1 cup milk
    4 egg yolks

Meringue Topping:
    4 egg whites
    8 tablespoons sugar

Preheat the oven to 400°. Poke a few holes in the pie crust. Bake the crust until golden brown.

Put the sugar, the butter, and the Half and Half in a the top of a double boiler over medium heat and cook it until it bubbles, gets thick and browns, about five minutes. Watch it closely because the syrup can burn. Then take it off the boiler bottom and set it to the side to cool a little bit.

In another bowl, mix the flour and the milk gradually until well blended. Beat the egg yolks in a separate bowl and put in the flour and milk. Stir that up real good. Put in the cooled syrup. Put it all back in the double boiler and let it cook until thick. That takes a little while. Be sure to stir it while it is cooking. Let the filling cool before putting it in the crust.

Beat the egg whites while gradually adding the sugar. When they are stiff, pour them on top of the butterscotch custard in the pie crust and put it in the oven at 350° for 15 minutes or until the meringue is golden brown.

Tart Lemon Meringue Pie

1 9" pie crust (see Five Pie Crusts recipe on page 90)

Filling:
  1 cup sugar
  5 tablespoons cornstarch
  1/8 teaspoon salt
  2 cups water
  3 eggs, separated
  3 tablespoons butter
  1/3 cup lemon juice
  2 teaspoons grated lemon rind

Meringue Topping:
  3 egg whites
  6 tablespoons sugar

Preheat the oven to 400°. Poke a few holes in the pie crust. Bake the crust until golden brown.

Mix together the sugar, cornstarch and salt in the top of a double boiler and then add the water. Cook the filling, stirring constantly over low heat until it thickens. Turn the heat up so that the water boils and cook for 10 more minutes. Take a few spoonfuls out of the filling and stir them into the beaten egg yolks. Then put the egg yolks in with the hot filling. Cook three minutes more. Then stir in the butter, lemon juice and rind. Take off the heat and let the filling cool. When it is cool, pour into the baked pie shell.

To make the meringue, beat the eggs until stiff, adding six tablespoons of sugar gradually. Pile on top of the filled pie shell. Bake at 350° for 15 to 20 minutes until the top of the meringue browns.

Chess Pie

"Beat the filling real good. The beating is the secret."

1 9" pie crust (see recipe for Five Pie Crusts on page 90)

Filling:
>   3 eggs, separated
>   3 whole eggs
>   2 cups sugar
>   1 stick (8 tablespoons) butter, softened
>   1 teaspoon white vinegar
>   1/2 cup Half and Half cream

Meringue Topping:
>   3 egg whites
>   6 tablespoons sugar

Preheat the oven to 350°.

Let the butter come to room temperature. Separate three eggs. Set the whites aside to be used later for the meringue. Add the three egg yolks to the three whole eggs and mix with the two cups of sugar and the stick of softened butter. Beat with a mixer until fluffy. Then add one teaspoon of white vinegar and the 1/2 cup of Half and Half. Beat. Pour the mixture into the prepared pie crust. Bake at 350° for 45 minutes or until firm in the center.

Just before the pie is ready to come out of the oven, beat the three egg whites with the six tablespoons of sugar, adding the sugar gradually. Pour the meringue mixture on top of the pie when it comes out of the oven. Then put the pie back in and bake it 15 more minutes at 350° or until golden brown on top.

Pecan Pie

"Now this is a real good pecan pie! Bake it until the bubble puffs up in the middle. If you cook it longer than this, the bubble drops back, and your filling will be too hard."

3/4 stick (6 tablespoons) butter, melted
3 eggs, beaten
1/2 cup white Karo Syrup
1 cup brown sugar
1 teaspoon vanilla
1 teaspoon vinegar
1 tablespoon flour
1 rounded cup of broken pecans
1 unbaked 9" pie shell (see Five Pie Crusts recipe on page 90)

Preheat the oven to 375°. Melt the butter. Add the beaten eggs. Add the syrup, brown sugar, vanilla, vinegar, and flour. Mix well. Pour in the unbaked pie shell. Top with nuts. Bake for 15 minutes, then turn down the oven to 350° and bake for approximately 20 minutes longer.

Thanksgiving

Turkey with Gravy and Dressing
Mashed Potatoes
Broccoli Casserole
Cranberry Salad
Rolls
Pecan Pie
Spiced Cider

Peach Cobbler

*"I can't go to the store without buying peaches. I peel,
slice, and freeze them. Then I have them for pies, 'cause
I don't like canned peach pie or cobbler."*

1 9" pie crust (see Five Pie Crusts recipe on page 90)
1/2 stick (4 tablespoons) butter
3 pounds or 4 cups fresh peaches
almond extract and lemon juice
1-1/2 cups sugar
1 tablespoon flour
1/2 stick butter, melted

Roll out the pie crust and put it in a deep baking dish, reserving the extra
dough for a criss-cross pattern on top of the cobbler. Dot with pieces of
butter on the bottom of the crust.

Peel and slice the peaches and mix them with a few drops of almond
extract and lemon juice. In a separate bowl mix the sugar and flour. Place
the peaches alternately with the sugar and flour mixture and then dots of
butter on top of the crust.

Cover top with strips of dough in a criss-cross pattern. Brush top with
melted butter if you want. Place the cobbler in a preheated 450° oven for
15 minutes. Then turn down the heat to 350° for another half hour or
until the cobbler bubbles up real good.

Blackberry Cobbler

1 9" pie crust (see Five Pie Crusts recipe on page 90)
1/2 stick (4 tablespoons) butter
2 cups sugar
4 tablespoons flour
dash of nutmeg
1 quart blackberries

Roll out the pie crust and put in a deep baking dish, reserving the extra dough for a criss-cross pattern on top of the cobbler. Dot the crust with butter. Mix up the sugar, flour and nutmeg. Place the blackberries alternately with the sugar and flour mixture and then dots of butter on top of the crust.

Cover top with strips of dough in a criss-cross pattern. Brush top with melted butter if you want. Place the cobbler in a preheated 450° oven for 15 minutes. Then turn down the heat to 350° for another half hour or until the cobbler bubbles up real good.

Summer Supper

Fried Chicken

Potato Salad

Layer Salad

Rolls

Blackberry Cobbler

Lemonade

Lemon Bars

"People are always calling for these. I make them every week for somebody."

Crust:

    2 sticks (1 cup) butter
    1/2 cup powdered sugar
    2 cups flour

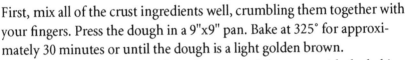

Filling:

    4 eggs
    2 cups sugar
    1 teaspoon baking powder
    4 tablespoons flour
    4 tablespoons lemon juice (or more to taste)
    grated lemon rind

First, mix all of the crust ingredients well, crumbling them together with your fingers. Press the dough in a 9"x9" pan. Bake at 325° for approximately 30 minutes or until the dough is a light golden brown.

While the crust is cooking, beat the eggs and the sugar with the baking powder, then add the flour, lemon juice and lemon rind. When the crust has baked, pour the filling over the top and return the pan to the oven. Bake for 25 more minutes or until golden brown. Don't overcook. They should be real soft. Remove the pan from the oven and while hot, sprinkle the top with powdered sugar. Cut into squares while barely warm.

Makes two dozen.

Dark Secrets

*"This is a good Christmas treat. It makes about 125
small cookies. You can sour milk on your own by adding
a tablespoon of vinegar to one cup of milk."*

2 sticks (1 cup) butter
3 cups brown sugar
4 tablespoons sour milk
4 eggs
6-1/4 cups flour
2 teaspoons baking soda
2 cups raisins
1 cup candied fruit
2 cups walnuts
3 teaspoons nutmeg
1 teaspoon cinnamon
2 tablespoons Maker's Mark bourbon

Cream the butter and the sugar together. Add the sour milk and the eggs. In a separate bowl, sift half of the flour and soda together, then add to the butter mixture. Then add the fruit and the nuts which have been chopped and floured with some of the flour called for in the recipe. Mix well. Sift the spices with the remaining flour and soda and then mix this with the dough. Add the bourbon. Mix well again.

Drop the dough with a teaspoon onto greased cookie sheets, leaving lots of space between each spoonful, as the cookies spread a lot upon baking. Bake eight minutes at 375°.

These can be made a long time in advance. Put them in a tin lined with foil. Soak a cloth in bourbon and lay on top. Slice up an apple on top of the cloth and close up your tin.

Butterscotch Squares

"They're right good!"

1 stick (8 tablespoons) butter	1 teaspoon baking powder
1 cup brown sugar	1 teaspoon vanilla
1 cup white sugar	1 cup pecans
4 eggs, well beaten	powdered sugar
1 cup flour	

Preheat the oven to 350°. Cream the butter and both sugars. Add the eggs. Put the baking powder in the flour. Add the flour to the butter-sugar-egg mixture. Add the vanilla and the nuts. Beat at low speed. Pour into a greased pan. Cook at 350° for 30 minutes. Cool. Cut and dust with powdered sugar.

Twice-Baked Pecan Squares

1 stick (8 tablespoons) butter or margarine, softened
1/2 cup firmly packed dark brown sugar
1 cup flour
2 eggs
1 cup firmly packed light brown sugar
1 cup chopped pecans
1/2 cup flaked coconut
2 tablespoons flour
1 teaspoon vanilla
pinch of salt
powdered sugar

Preheat the oven to 350°. Cream together the softened butter and the dark brown sugar. Add the cup of flour and mix well. Press into a 13"x9"x2" pan and bake for 10-20 minutes or until crispy and golden brown.

Beat together the eggs until frothy. Add the light brown sugar and beat until smooth and thickened. In a separate bowl, combine the pecans, the coconut, and the two tablespoons of flour. Then mix with the egg and sugar, and add the vanilla and salt. Stir well and spread over the cooked crust. Bake again at 350° for 10 to 20 minutes. Cool. Sprinkle lightly with powdered sugar. Cut into squares.

Makes three to four dozen squares.

Pecan Tarts

"I make them all the time. A great favorite of Jim Thomas'!"

Tart shells:
>   1 (3 ounce) package of cream cheese
>   1 cup flour
>   1 stick (8 tablespoons) butter

Mix together the ingredients, then divide the dough in half, and then divide each half into six balls. Line 12 greased muffin tins with the dough by pressing it in place with your fingers and place the tins in refrigerator while fixing the filling.

Filling:
>   3 eggs
>   1/2 cup sugar
>   1 tablespoon melted butter
>   1/4 teaspoon salt
>   1 cup light corn syrup
>   1 teaspoon vanilla
>   3/4 cup chopped pecans

Preheat the oven to 350°. Mix all of the ingredients. Fill the muffin tins 3/4 full using a tablespoon. Bake for 30 minutes. Remove from oven. Let the tarts stand a few minutes before taking out them of the tins.

Double Chocolate Brownies

"When you make the icing it tries to get too hard on you. That's the problem. Beat it until melted and smooth."

1 stick (8 tablespoons) butter
1 cup sugar
4 eggs
1 teaspoon vanilla
1 can Hersheys chocolate syrup
1 cup and 1 tablespoon flour
1/2 teaspoon baking powder
1/2 cup nuts (optional)

Beat together the butter and the sugar. Add the eggs, two at a time. Add the vanilla and chocolate syrup. Add the flour, baking powder, and nuts. Put in a 11"x15" greased pan. Bake at 350° for 30 minutes.

Icing:
6 tablespoons butter
6 tablespoons milk
1-1/2 cups sugar
1/2 cup chocolate chips

Boil the butter, milk and sugar for 30 seconds. Add the chocolate chips. Beat until melted and smooth. Spread on the hot brownies.

Crème De Menthe Bars

1 stick (8 tablespoons) butter, softened
l cup sugar
4 eggs
1 cup flour
1/2 teaspoon salt
1 (16 ounce) can chocolate syrup
1 teaspoon vanilla

Cream the butter, then gradually add the sugar, beating until light and fluffy. Add the eggs, one at a time, beating well after each addition. Combine the flour and salt; add these to the creamed mixture alternately with the chocolate syrup, beginning and ending with the flour mixture. Add the vanilla. Pour the batter into a greased and floured 13"x9"x2" baking pan. Bake at 350° for 25-28 minutes. Cool completely before spreading with frosting and glaze. (Cake will shrink from the sides of the pan.)

Frosting:
1/2 stick (4 tablespoons) butter, softened
2 cups sifted powdered sugar
2 tablespoons crème de menthe

Cream the butter. Gradually add the sugar and the crème de menthe, mixing well. Spread evenly over the cake. Top with chocolate glaze.

Chocolate Glaze:
1 (6 ounce) package semi-sweet chocolate bits
1/2 (4 tablespoons) stick butter

Combine the chocolate bits and butter in the top of a double boiler. Bring the water to a boil. Reduce the heat to low, stir until the chocolate melts. Spread over the frosted cake. Chill about one hour before cutting into squares.

Meringues

"You can serve anything with these. They're good with ice cream, or fresh peaches, or strawberries and whipped cream, or lemon custard. You can use the lemon custard recipe from the Lemon Meringue Pie or the Angel Pie recipes."

4 egg whites
1 teaspoon vinegar
1/2 teaspoon cream of tartar
1-1/2 cups white sugar
powdered sugar

Preheat the oven to 275°. Mix the vinegar and the cream of tartar into the egg whites and beat the whites until stiff. Gradually add the sugar, beating. Put a brown paper sack on a baking sheet (make sure there is no writing on the sack), and sprinkle with powdered sugar. Drop the meringue batter by spoonfuls onto the paper. Bake for 45 minutes.

Makes about 12 meringues, depending on the size of the spoonful.

Beverages

Slush Punch

"I use this for all kinds of occasions when people call for punch. It seems to be especially nice for weddings because it's pink."

3-1/2 cups sugar
6 cups water
6 ounces of Mixed Fruit Jello
1 quart pineapple juice
1 quart orange juice
2/3 cup lemon juice
2 (28 ounce) bottles of ginger ale, chilled

Mix the sugar and water in a sauce pan and boil. Then simmer about three minutes. Put in the Jello and stir until it dissolves. Remove the pan from the heat and mix in the fruit juices. Pour in a large container and freeze. Several hours before serving, take the container out and let the punch soften. Put the slush in your bowl and pour the ginger ale on top to serve.

Wedding Reception

Roast Beef on Buns with Mustard Sauce
Ham Biscuits
Turkey Sandwiches
Vegetable Dip
Asparagus Rolls
Shrimp Mold
Cheese Tray with Crackers
Fresh Fruit
Wedding Cake and Groom's Cake
Slush Punch

Spiced Cider

"October is a good month for fresh cider. This is nice to serve during the Fall and Christmas holidays"

1 gallon apple cider
3/4 cup orange juice
3/4 cup sugar
2 teaspoons whole allspice
2 teaspoons whole cloves
2 sticks cinnamon

Completely dissolve the sugar and the orange juice in the cider before pouring it in an electric coffee maker. Put your spices in the basket and perk.

Serves 30.

Afternoon Tea

Benedictine

Pimiento Cheese

Chicken Salad Sandwiches

Ham Biscuits

Lemon Bars

Double Chocolate Brownies

Spiced Cider

Susanna Thomas was born in New York City and grew up in the nearby Hudson River valley town of Irvington, New York. She received an A.B. degree in Comparative Literature from Princeton University. After graduation, she worked at Random House publishers in Manhattan. In 1984, to pursue a life-long interest in horses, Mrs. Thomas moved to the Bluegrass area of Kentucky to work on Thoroughbred farms. In the last ten years, she has written numerous articles for equine publications. She lives on a farm in Mercer County with her husband and son.

Mrs. Thomas' interest in good food harks back to her Swiss grandparents and mother, all excellent cooks, and to the years Mrs. Thomas spent as a young girl living in the gastronomic haven of Paris, France. Mrs. Thomas is intrigued by all sorts of cuisines, enjoys experimenting in the kitchen, and loves to entertain.

Thelma's Treasures

The Secret Recipes of "The Best Cook in Harrodsburg"

by Susanna Thomas

If you treasure this cookbook and would like another to give or to keep, additional copies may be obtained by using the order form provided below, and mailing it with your check or money order to:

LITTLE BARTER PRESS
465 Balden Lane, Harrodsburg, KY 40330
*Allow 3-4 weeks for delivery.

cut here

SEND TO:

Name _____

Address _____

City _____ *State* _____ *Zip* _____

_____ *Copies at $10.00 each*

Kentucky residents add 6% sales tax or 60 cents
Add $2.00 for the first copy for postage and handling.
Add $1.00 per copy for each additional copy.

Enclosed is a check or money order for _____

cut here

SEND TO:

Name _____

Address _____

City _____ *State* _____ *Zip* _____

_____ *Copies at $10.00 each*

Kentucky residents add 6% sales tax or 60 cents
Add $2.00 for the first copy for postage and handling.
Add $1.00 per copy for each additional copy.

Enclosed is a check or money order for _____

Notes